Please return or renew this item by the last date shown.
Fines will be charged if the book is kept after this date.
Thank you for using *your* library.

 100% recycled paper.

Dear Pitman Publishing Customer

IMPORTANT – Read This Now!

We are delighted to announce a special free service for all of our customers.

Simply complete this form and return it to the address overleaf to receive:

A Free Customer Newsletter

B Free Information Service

C Exclusive Customer Offers – which have included free software, videos and relevant products

D Opportunity to take part in product development sessions

E The chance for you to write about your own business experience and become one of our respected authors

Fill this in now and return it to us (no stamp needed in the UK) to join our customer information service.

Name: Position:

Company/Organisation:

Address (including postcode):

                                         Country:

Telephone: Fax:

Nature of business:

Title of book purchased:

Comments:

-------------------------------- **Fold Here Then Staple** --------------------------------

We would be very grateful if you could answer these questions to help us with market research.

1   Where/How did you hear of this book?

☐ in a bookshop

☐ in a magazine/newspaper
(please state which):

☐ information through the post

☐ recommendation from a colleague

☐ other (please state which):

2   Which newspaper(s)/magazine(s) do you read regularly?:

3   When buying a business book which factors influence you most?
(Please rank in order)

☐ recommendation from a colleague

☐ price

☐ content

☐ recommendation in a bookshop

☐ author

☐ publisher

☐ title

☐ other(s):

4   Is this book a

☐ personal purchase?

☐ company purchase?

5   Would you be prepared to spend a few minutes talking to our customer services staff to help with product development? YES/NO

The Business Publisher

Written for managers competing in today's tough business world, our books will help you get the edge on competitors by showing you how to:

- increase quality, efficiency and productivity throughout your organisation
- use both proven and innovative management techniques
- improve the management skills of you and your staff
- implement winning customer strategies

In short they provide concise, practical information that you can use every day to improve the success of your business.

FINANCIAL TIMES
PITMAN PUBLISHING

the Institute of Management
FOUNDATION
PITMAN PUBLISHING

WC2E 9BR, UK
LONDON
128 Long Acre
FREEPOST
Pitman Professional Publishing
Free Information Service

No stamp
necessary
in the UK

Cash is King

Cash is King

A Practical Guide to Strategic Cash Management

KEITH CHECKLEY

FINANCIAL TIMES

PITMAN PUBLISHING

PITMAN PUBLISHING
128 Long Acre, London WC2E 9AN

A Division of Longman Group Limited

First published in Great Britain 1994

A CIP catalogue record for this book can be obtained from the British Library.

ISBN 0 273 60465 1

Typeset by PanTek Arts, Maidstone, Kent
Printed and bound in Great Britain by Biddles Ltd, Guildford and King's Lynn

The Publishers' policy is to use paper manufactured from sustainable forests

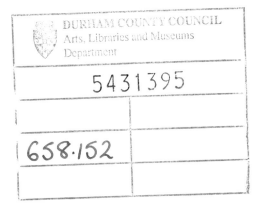

CONTENTS

- NWA Survey data – 450 companies
- Capital expenditure: introduction to methods of appraisal
- Monitoring liquidity
- Critical analysis of variations
- Liquidity out of control
- Cash receipts from break-up values

ACKNOWLEDGEMENTS

I am particularly grateful to Timothy H. Jury FCA for his invaluable assistance with this book and his contribution on 'cash flow – its place within business'. To Keith Dickinson FCIB for his work on contrasting cash flow profiles and working investment calculations with case-study profiles. To Rick Shobbrook, Standard Chartered Bank, Head of Group Risk Training and his colleague Bob Graham for their original idea of using Hi-Tec Sports plc as a case study demonstrating cash flow management issues.

I need to thank members of the Pitman team and particularly David Crosby and Richard Stagg. Also Trish, Laura and Sue for excellent editing work and Claire for her encouragement to complete this very demanding project.

Finally thanks to Brian Clifford of Manchester Business School for research on the American scene and to Marcus Nidd for research but more particularly for the superb graphics work.

Keith Checkley

INTRODUCTION

CASH IS KING!!

The strategic management of cash flow is essential to the survival of any business, be it large or small. Cash is the fuel to drive the business – without it the business will certainly fail . . .

Extract from *Financial Times* 22/2/91

CASH FLOW BECOMES THE DETERMINING FACTOR

by David Waller and Maggie Urry

With UK corporate finances coming under pressure in the recession, attention is focusing on companies' ability to generate cash. It is, after all, cash which pays the dividends. And since companies are essentially rated by the stock market on the basis of their future dividend paying potential, cash flow is a vital measure of corporate financial health.

The stock market has not in the past put much emphasis on judging companies by their cash generating ability. Analysts have traditionally assessed a company's performance in terms of a handful of simple yardsticks, with most emphasis put on the price/earnings per share ratio.

But these measures have become less reliable in recent years, as companies have become more creative in their accounting practices.

The collapse of a number of quoted companies, which from the balance sheets appeared healthy, has added to concern. As the cash squeeze on companies has tightened, many have looked to ways to conserve cash, such as cutting back on investment or squeezing their suppliers in turn.

'There have been too many surprises,' reflects one analyst. 'Throughout the 1980s companies tested the accounting rules to the limit. You just cannot afford to take a set of accounts on trust.'

This makes a company's cash flow a more important investment yardstick. As UBS Phillips & Drew conclude in a report on the UK corporate sector's favoured accounting tricks, 'whereas manufacturing profits is relatively easy, cash flow is the most difficult parameter to adjust in a company's accounts.'

►

They add 'we believe that there should be less emphasis placed on the reported progression of earnings per share and more attention paid to balance sheet potential, and most importantly of all, cash.'

The problem is, as analysts at Laing & Cruickshank, the brokers, point out, 'the conventional description of cash flow is an optimistic measure.' It is simply retained profits plus depreciation.

However, this figure can be boosted by non-trading items such as the profit on the sale of assets, or by capitalising interest, making the interest charge in the profit and loss account lower than the actual cash going out to a company's banks. Further the treatment of associates' profits means that a company's pre-tax profits are boosted by an amount larger than the dividend which is received from the associates.

L&C has developed a system of comparing a company's traditional cash flow with their profit records, and applied it to the leading quoted companies. This throws up some interesting examples. Companies which are spending heavily on expansion may appear to have fast growing pre-tax profits. But they can be draining away cash as they spend more than they earn.

Unfortunately, these attempts to look at trading cash flow are far more complex than the simple price/earnings ratio. However, within a couple of months the job of assessing cash flows should become easier when the Accounting Standards Board, the arbiter of UK accounting rules, publishes a new standard FRS1 requiring companies to publish cash flow statements instead of statements showing the source and application of funds, which show movements in all working capital rather than just cash.

The new standard has yet to be finalised but it is likely that companies will have to show cash coming from operating, investing, and financing activities. This may allow analysts to develop a new measure for rating shares based on trading cash flow.

Extract from the Chief Executive

'Great news! Our sales have almost doubled this month and we expect to make a profit of around £100,000.'

The Finance Director

'Sorry, Sir – the bank's been on the telephone, we are in excess, I don't know if they will pay our wages cheque this Friday!'

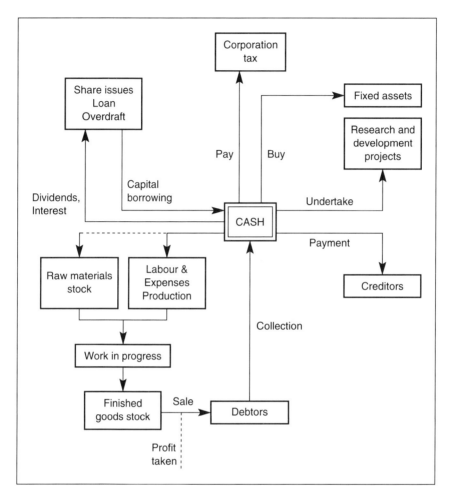

Fig 1.1 The Capital Cycle

Cash can be seen, in this illustration, as the central hub of the capital cycle. Cash is needed to continually finance the asset conversion cycle, to enable payments to the bank, to pay dividends to the shareholders, to pay taxes due, to purchase further fixed assets and to undertake research and development, etc.

Let us begin our CASH FLOW book by looking in Chapter One at the place of cash flow within business, and endeavouring to plot a more steady course for the cash flow direction of our business.

1

CASH FLOW – ITS PLACE WITHIN BUSINESS

INTRODUCTION TO CASH FLOW

Traditionally, most emphasis has been placed on the identification of profit and loss and the asset position of a business in providing financial information about it. Until relatively recently both the public disclosure and taxation requirements were served by the preparation of statutory accounts consisting mainly of a profit and loss account and balance sheet. In the last decade, however, awareness has developed amongst informed users of the need for more relevant information regarding cash flows.

This is not, however, the main reason for requiring an understanding of cash flow. Over the last 30 years we have seen the development of an increasingly fast moving and volatile business environment. The cyclical nature of markets and economies has made the accurate prediction of cash flows the single most important management weapon in the avoidance of corporate mishap and the controlled delivery of corporate performance.

In order to competently manage the cash flow of a business it is first necessary to develop a thorough understanding of the various components which make up the flow of cash through the business.

Fundamentally, business is an extremely straightforward activity. First ask yourself this: **What is the motivation to trade?**

The answer in most cases is to make money, or to put it another way – *generate a surplus cash flow*. The second key question is: **How do we do this?**

Again the answer appears obvious and a little simplistic – *by buying and selling things*. The cash flows involved in buying and selling things are the root cause of the problems associated with the control of cash flows, *irrespective of the profitability or otherwise of the undertaking involved*. This is where the identification of profit and loss and the prediction of future cash

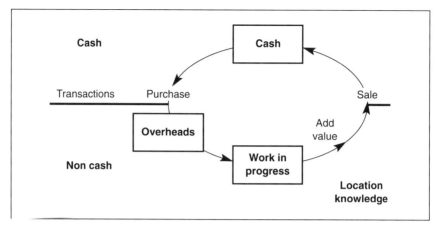

Fig 1.1 The Simplest Business: The Trader

flows part ways in terms of their relative importance to the survival of any business.

Before considering the usual methods of predicting the cash flows of a business it is necessary to establish and confirm our understanding of the various elements which make up the cash flows of a typical business. A manufacturing business represents the most complex general case. Retail and service businesses are simpler in concept. The differences will be discussed in more detail later.

THE SIMPLEST BUSINESS

The simplest business of all is that of the trader who buys and sells without doing anything to the item traded. He is adding value by moving the item from a place of surplus to one where there is a demand, or he is utilising his knowledge to sell the item for more than he paid for it.

Such a business can be represented in Fig 1.1.

Using cash the trader makes a purchase and some time later resells the item acquired for more than he paid for it, receiving cash in exchange for the item.

This is effectively all a retail or distribution business does, repeating the above cycle many times and adding value by relocating goods to a position where there is adequate demand for them.

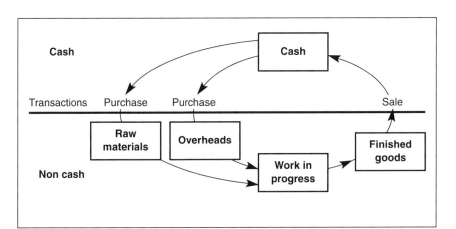

Fig 1.2 The Next Simplest Business: The Manufacturer

THE NEXT SIMPLEST BUSINESS

The next simplest business is one where the trader does work to the item purchased before reselling it. Such a business can be represented as shown in Figure 1.2.

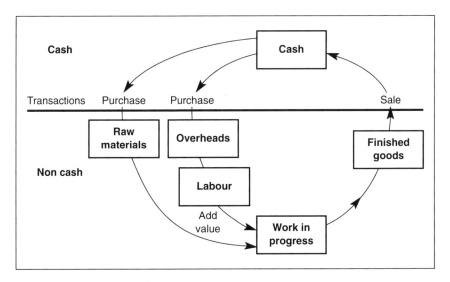

Fig 1.3 The Next Simplest Business 2

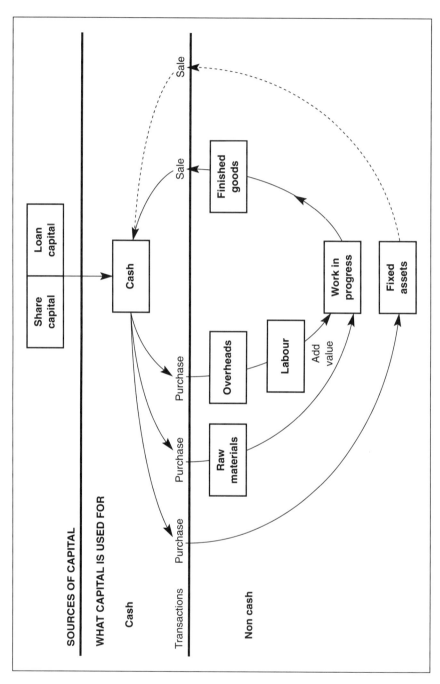

Fig 1.4 The Next Simplest Business 3

Using cash the trader makes a purchase of raw materials and does work on them, consuming overheads in the process. An example might be a furniture manufacturer buying wood and working on this to create a piece of furniture. This is the most simplistic representation of a manufacturing business.

Let us further develop our example and assume that our furniture manufacturer is sufficiently successful that he decides to take on helpers. The business then looks like Fig 1.3.

Labour now joins overheads as an item purchased by the business to add value to raw materials.

Our model is still simplistic. Let us assume our furniture manufacturer continues to prosper. He now wishes to make the business independent of himself (perhaps by forming a company), so that he can borrow money and buy machinery to further add value to his products.

Our model now looks like Fig 1.4.

The business is now separate from the trader and is obtaining the cash it needs to trade by issuing shares and borrowing money. In addition to the cash being used to buy raw materials and pay for overheads and labour some of it is now used to buy machinery and possibly other fixed assets.

THE REAL BUSINESS MODEL

Our model is now almost complete. There is one key deficiency however, we have not recognised the effect of time on the cash flows of our business.

There is often a difference between the time we take physical delivery of something we have purchased and when we pay for it. Conversely it is common to sell something to a customer allowing them a period of time to pay, the cash due for the product being received some time later. These time delays have a substantial effect on a business and must therefore be incorporated in our model. Our model has now evolved as shown in Figure 1.5.

Two new boxes have appeared labelled creditors and debtors. Creditors are people who the business owes cash to; debtors are people who owe cash to the business.

We can now reconsider what happens to cash within a business.

Our business purchases raw materials and pays for overheads and labour from suppliers who do not expect payment for one to two months. They are creditors of the business during this period, effectively loaning cash to the business.

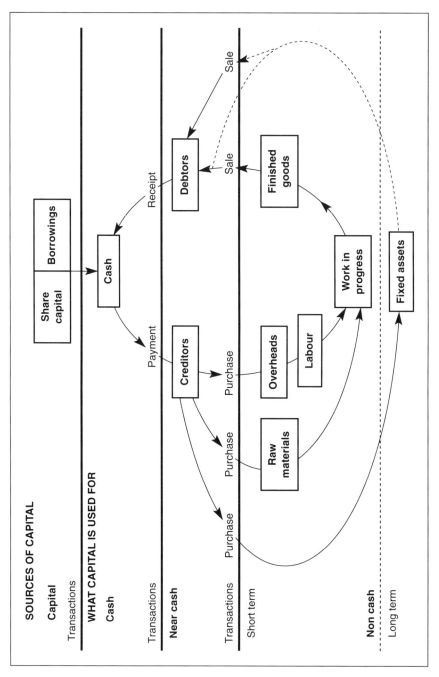

Fig 1.5 The Real Business Model

The business then adds value to the raw materials to create finished goods which are sold to customers to yield a surplus. The customers may not pay the business for one to two months. Eventually they do and cash is received which is used to pay creditors. This cycle is known as the WORKING CAPITAL CYCLE and is the most active and volatile flow of cash funds through most businesses. It is the most demanding area of cash management to control.

THE COMPLETE REAL BUSINESS MODEL

Our model is now almost complete. We see the WORKING CAPITAL CYCLE, we see cash purchasing FIXED ASSETS and we see the sources of cash – these being SHARE CAPITAL and BORROWINGS.

There are two further elements to add to make the model reasonably representative of most businesses. Both of these are concerned with the surplus of cash which we will have created if we have traded successfully. It will come as no surprise to you that this is known as profit.

Our complete model is as shown in Figure 1.6.

To complete the model two further boxes have been added. Investments in the centre represents the transfer of cash not needed in the WORKING CAPITAL CYCLE or for the purchase of FIXED ASSETS to a deposit account or perhaps into gilts or some other short term interest earning investment. This is usually CASH that is SURPLUS to requirements in the short term (timing affecting the business again) but which may be needed later.

The dividends, interest, taxation box represents the payment *out* of the business of the surpluses or profit generated by trading to the shareholders and providers of borrowings (usually banks).

Implications of the model in managing cash flows

The model provides a framework to assimilate the components of the cash flows of a business. From the model we can see that most businesses are investing cash in an endless procession through creditors, into stock and work-in-progress and eventually finished goods, whereupon, following a sale of the item involved, becoming a debtor and then back to cash.

Experienced managers will know that this journey is fraught with difficulty. Problems can be experienced with the quality and performance of the inputs to the manufacturing process – usually raw materials, labour and overheads. Having assembled the relevant components in one place the

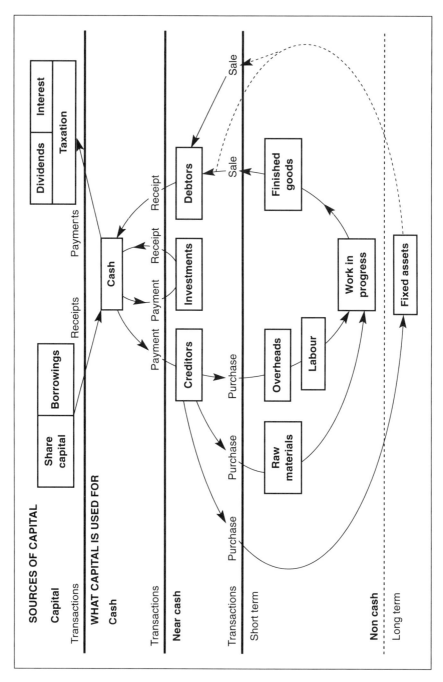

Fig 1.6 The Complete Real Business Model

manufacturing process has to take place correctly with the right goods being manufactured at the right time without any of the problems associated with a failure to maintain quality. These processes alone represent a logistical nightmare in all but the smallest company.

Finally the goods require packaging and storage prior to despatch to their customer. Only then can the business raise an invoice to create the debtor which will, in the absence of customer credit problems, turn into cash.

All these problems however fade into insignificance when compared with the problems caused by time!

You may be wondering what time has to do with this. **Timing is the essence of working capital management**, which in turn is the key component of cash flow management. Let us take two examples.

Sainsbury plc orders a truckload of beans from Heinz plc on day one. The beans arrive at Sainsbury's distribution depot on day three and arrive in the store on days four. On days five, six and seven the beans are sold for cash to customers. Thus, Sainsbury have made their journey round the working capital cycle in about a week.

Contrast this with British Aerospace plc who are constructing a fighter aircraft for Saudi Arabia. Following years of negotiation BAe receives an order for a number of aircraft. This in turn initiates the thousands of orders necessary to obtain the various components and sub-assemblies required from their respective suppliers. Over a period of many months the aircraft is assembled (being work in progress at this point), completed and tested (becoming finished goods at this point). Finally after further performance tests by the Saudis the plane is accepted into service and paid for. This journey round the working capital cycle takes many months, possibly years.

What conclusion can we draw from these admittedly extreme examples? If Sainsbury's agrees 60 day settlement terms with Heinz they will be able to sell the goods and hold the resultant cash for around 50 days before settling their liability to Heinz. In other words Sainsbury plc *generates cash from trading*, it enjoys the benefits of a *negative* working capital cycle. The more trade *increases* the more cash is generated.

British Aerospace enjoys a much less favourable outcome. They have to invest many millions of pounds in the working capital cycle to manufacture each fighter aircraft. The funding of the working capital alone on such large contracts is a major undertaking. The more successful BAe is the more money has to be found to invest in working capital. *Increased trading causes more cash to be absorbed into the working capital cycle.*

MANAGING THE ELEMENTS OF THE CASH FLOW CYCLE

It follows that the first key to the control of working capital is to *minimise the amount invested* in the working capital cycle. We shall now look in more detail at what this means for each component of the model.

Creditors

Creditors are unusual in that during the period of credit taken they represent an interest free loan to the company, the benefit of which arises directly as a consequence of trading. Thus it is in the interests of most businesses to maximise the free credit period available from creditors. This does not necessarily mean extending the period before payment beyond the terms agreed with creditors as this will impact on the business in three ways. It will affect its credit rating adversely, it could result in suppliers increasing prices to compensate for the funding cost of the delayed payment and finally creditors may withdraw from supplying whilst taking action to place the business into bankruptcy.

Where creditworthiness is not an issue, considerable scope may exist to negotiate extended terms with key suppliers, particularly if your business is a large or particularly strategic customer for the creditor supplier. This can be particularly beneficial if more traditional forms of lending, such as bank loans, are difficult to obtain.

Labour

Labour costs are usually the second biggest input into the manufacturing process after raw materials: consequently the sums involved can be substantial. There are a variety of strategies available to the business experiencing problems ranging from a temporary cut in wages imposed across the board to substantial redundancies across all functions within the business. There is usually also considerable scope to temporarily defer the paying over of deductions to the government although this is increasingly the subject of ever more onerous legislation introducing and extending the penalties involved and giving the recipient government department the right to charge interest. Accordingly such actions should only be contemplated after taking appropriate advice regarding the risks involved.

Overheads

Overheads are the remaining component of expenditure in all businesses. There is usually considerable scope to cut overheads in most businesses experiencing a shortfall of cash for the first time. The larger the business the more redundant expenditure will be discovered which no one will previously have had the time to examine and eliminate.

For the purpose of a more detailed examination overheads can be split into various generic types.

Establishment expenses

These represent the costs of occupation of property. A variety of strategies are available here. These range from the reduction in the space occupied within a building, offering the option of renting off or selling the surplus space; to the elimination for as long as is necessary of all non-essential costs such as gardening, office cleaning, decoration and non-essential maintenance.

Production expenses

Production costs require constant review if a business is to remain absolutely competitive at all times. Where this process has been neglected technology may provide numerous opportunities to substitute newer, faster machinery to replace older more cumbersome machinery employing more people to operate. Using hire-purchase finance it may be possible to reduce costs substantially without *any* direct cash outflow. This method is particularly effective where the demand for the product manufactured is fairly consistent.

Measuring the output of labour is particularly important. If this is not done you will find that the time required to complete work always expands to match the paid hours available. The introduction of labour productivity measurement alone can result in significant increases in productivity as can the monitoring of all reasons for any non-productive time arising each working week.

An analysis of maintenance costs can reveal much useful information and expose specific machines and operations which may be absorbing disproportionate amounts of maintenance time and effort. Simply ceasing to use such machines may be possible, or alternatively minor modifications or reorganisation may also be sufficient to save much wasted resource and time.

A thorough review of all the components of production costs may expose areas where an item or service might be more cheaply sourced outside the business. If whole departments can be dispensed with this has other knock-on effects such as improving the focus of the business and simplifying its management.

Selling expenses

It is important to ensure that the costs of marketing and selling the business's output are fairly matched to the areas of strategic margin generation. It is possible that the traditional markets served by the business have been superseded by newer markets without any refocusing of the business's sales resource.

Administration expenses

In times of cash crisis and difficulties with liquidity and cash flow the administrative areas of the company come under increasing pressure to perform better with less and less resource. Capital expenditure and discretionary expenses are cut and there is an increased need for cash flow management, information and control. Paradoxically this usually means it may be necessary to add resource to the administration function rather than remove it. Liquidity problems usually arise due to lack of management foresight, and consequently in such companies there are often no budgets or forecasts. These must be prepared as the problems develop, in addition to the cash flow information mentioned earlier, so further stretching what is likely by this point to be an insufficient resource within the administration function.

Financing costs

These are generally determined when a business first enters into financing arrangements – usually in better times! However, there may be scope for re-negotiation of the detail of an arrangement as it is usually in the interest of lenders to assist the company in putting behind it any short term problem. There is often scope for reduction in the fees and charges associated with certain types of lending such as factoring, invoice discounting and even simple overdraft lending if there are many immediate transfer type of payments.

Stocks

Stocks represent the monetary way of identifying the value invested in the real or non-cash items within a business. Again there are certain imperatives to consider when reviewing any situation where working capital needs appear to become excessive. Let us consider the constituent parts of stocks.

RAW MATERIALS

These represent the basic material inputs to any manufacturing process. The first thing to consider is whether purchasing is under control. Who can purchase and what can they purchase? Where purchasing is not in control cash can easily be squandered in buying the wrong thing, buying too much of a thing, buying at the wrong time (usually too early but sometimes too late!), and buying at the wrong price. It is important to remember that a liability is incurred when a contract is entered into (i.e. when the order is given to the supplier), *not* when the cheque is signed.

WORK IN PROGRESS AND FINISHED GOODS

It is important to regularly review that both work in progress and finished goods are what they say they are, as opposed to work not in progress and finished things the business is unable to sell. Add to this things the business has bought but can't use – otherwise known as raw materials which are no use – and it is easy to see where cash can be invested into the working capital cycle never to reappear as cash again.

The key control here is regular stocktaking. This tells us two things, firstly that the stock we thought we had is still actually there and secondly how long we have had everything in stock and work in progress. The older stock is, the less likely it is to be sold for cash at anything near its real value. Provisions are commonly made in accounts for slow moving, obsolete and damaged stocks. In cash flow terms, all of them represent mistakes or lack of foresight on the part of management. Again many businesses neglect to properly review stocks and take appropriate action on their findings.

Fixed assets

The other major area of non-cash investment is of course fixed assets. The usual response to problems with cash flows is to put an embargo on all capital expenditure. If the company or group involved is relatively well invested this may not cause too many problems. However, it can be counter productive in companies where new investment may be the only way of improving performance in the short term. In larger manufacturing businesses it is common to find a substantial amount of non-essential machinery has been retained because it might come in useful in the future, or because it may yield spares for other machinery. Selling off non-essential machinery can often yield a useful cash contribution.

The premises occupied by the business can also provide a useful cash gain if necessary by downsizing or relocation of the existing business or sale and leaseback arrangements. If surplus space can be split off it may be possible to rent it out. Finally there may be development value in old premises, particularly if situated strategically to large centres of population.

Debtors

Finally we come to the last element of the model prior to the realisation of goods back into cash. Here the first thing to consider is speed of collection. Is it reasonable? Can it be improved? In the UK a reasonable collection is anything from 45 to 75 days depending on the typical industry payment terms and quality of the customer covenant. Numerous methods can be used to chase debt including dedicated credit controllers, extensive use of the telephone, and suing promptly in the last resort. More subtle is to consider carefully if the terms of business can be modified to provide more customer incentive to pay promptly, or whether improvements can be obtained by more effective forms of distribution to the end user of the product. It may be possible to control distribution more carefully so that customers generate more margin from the product sold – improving their cash flow and ability to pay. Finally it may be possible to sell a product for cash rather than on credit by changes in the product offering.

Whilst it would be possible to write a separate book on the control of each element within the cash flow model the key issues noted provide the outline of a strategy with which to attack the more common problems which arise with cash flows.

ANTICIPATING THE LIKELY BEHAVIOUR OF CASH FLOWS

The second key component of managing cash flows is to understand the pattern of the working capital behaviour of the business in which we are interested. This will enable us to anticipate the likely problems in control and management which might arise.

You will recollect the two examples earlier illustrating the difference in trading cash flow behaviour of Sainsbury's, a large food retailer, and British

Aerospace, a heavy engineering business. Each generic sector of the economy has a typical general pattern to its cash flow behaviour. This is largely driven by which part of the supply chain achieves the best added value between the origination of the raw materials involved and the end user of the goods or services involved. To put it another way, who enjoys the highest profitability within the supply chain. Secondly, competitive conditions within the industry will also have a marked effect on working capital norms.

It is important to assimilate what the normal behaviours of cash flow should be in your particular business. If for non-competitive reasons you have too much invested in the working capital cycle this represents a real cost disadvantage, particularly if you are borrowing to fund it.

Generally cash flows by sector look like this:

Retail

Retail splits into two types, fast moving and other. Retail businesses with fast moving stocks such as supermarkets, fast food outlets, newsagents, etc. generally enjoy a *negative* cash flow position, with creditors funding the entire working capital need and in many cases generating a surplus. They generate cash as they grow. Other retailers are generally businesses who enjoy success because they have a particular speciality stock such as clothes, housewares, jewellery, antiques etc., and thus have a *positive* working capital position because they carry extensive, slower moving stocks.

Manufacturing

Manufacturing also splits into two types, light manufacturing and heavy manufacturing. Light manufacturing businesses may operate with high volumes of smaller product. There may be considerable scope for them to use just-in-time manufacturing principles to minimise investment in stocks, so keeping working capital investment to a minimum. Heavy engineering by contrast usually involves massive amounts of working capital because of the inevitably slow pace of production. Generally, for all manufacturers, any reduction in the time period of production should yield benefits in reducing the amounts invested in working capital.

Service businesses usually carry little in the way of stocks, their primary means of adding value involving the consumption of labour and overheads. Much depends on whether the enterprise is a cash business or one where the customer pays on credit. If it is a cash business the working capital investment can often be negative. If credit is involved working capital funding can often be necessary.

Mining, timber, metals and other raw material and commodity businesses are characterised by massive initial capital investments to secure or create the source of the raw materials. Their working capital requirements are governed by the volumes of production and the relationship between costs and the price the commodity can reach on the open market.

As you can see from these principal generic examples it is possible to deduce the anticipated behaviour of the working capital flows for any business and hence the overall anticipated behaviour of cash flows. The key elements are the speed with which cash moves around the working capital cycle (usually expressed in debtor days, creditor days and stock days) and the volumes of the goods or services involved.

ASSESSING THE VULNERABILITY OF CASH FLOWS

The third key issue is to understand the appearance of a business whose cash flows are vulnerable to deterioration. The cash flows of any business can be summarised very elegantly in the following style:

Descriptions	Success Ltd £'000	Struggler Ltd £'000	Failure Ltd First Glance £'000	Failure Ltd Reality £'000
CASH GENERATION				
Cash from operations	2,000	1,000	500	500
Working capital investment	(500)	(700)	(700)	100
Fixed asset investment	(300)	(300)	(300)	(300)
Funding costs	(450)	(500)	(550)	(550)
Taxation and dividends	(250)			
Cash generated/absorbed	500	(500)	(1,050)	(250)
FUNDING MOVEMENT				
Short debt increase/decrease	(350)	350	800	
Long debt increase/decrease	(150)	150	250	250
Equity increase/decrease				
Other non-trading flows				
Net funding movement	(500)	500	1,050	250

As you can see Success Ltd is a positive cash generator. From the £2,000,000 cash generated from operations there is sufficient to invest £500,000 into the working capital cycle, £300,000 into fixed assets, £450,000 in interest to debt providers, pay £250,000 in tax and dividends and still have a surplus of £500,000 to reduce debt and increase cash reserves.

Struggler Ltd is achieving a poorer result. It is having to invest a net £500,000 more in working capital, fixed assets and debt servicing than it is generating from trading. If this is a recent and temporary reduction in earnings the company should not suffer too much. If, however, this is a pattern which has remained present for two or three years serious problems are likely to be present. No company can trade like this indefinitely. It eventually runs out of cash or debt capacity and becomes bankrupt. The management of Struggler Ltd need to take rapid and decisive action to solve their problems.

Failure Ltd has serious problems right now. It is not generating sufficient funds to cover its debt servicing costs. This is before even considering the sums expended into working capital and fixed assets in the current year. Debt is increasing massively to fund the under-performance. In reality of course such companies are often at the limits of their ability to borrow money in which case the cash flows look like the last column of the above example entitled Failure Ltd – Reality. The under-performance is resulting in a cash flow squeeze which manifests itself primarily in ever increasing creditors. These are used to subsidise the deterioration in stock and debtor position. It is possible to detect this situation by examining the number of days in the working capital cycle creditors represent, compared to the cost of sales. If this figure is between 75 and 115 days the company is operating in an extreme and very vulnerable creditor position.

The above summary of cash generation (or the lack of it) represents an extremely useful and brief way of demonstrating the cash generation performance of any business. It can be easily constructed from the information in the cash flow statement disclosed in the statutory accounts of UK based businesses. If this is not available then it can be deduced from the balance sheets at the beginning and end of the period under examination.

ASSESSING THE VOLATILITY OF CASH FLOWS

It is important to identify which are the most volatile areas of a business's cash flows. The cash generation report above summarises the principal areas of cash generation and investment. Generally most areas behave fairly consistently; most manufacturing and service businesses tend to see fairly steady cash generation from trading, construction businesses being the main generic group suffering volatility at this level. The most volatile area by far comes from movements in the working capital cycle; this being made up of swings in the value of debtors, stocks and creditors.

   Let us consider a sensitivity analysis of the values involved for a typical mature manufacturing business.

Typical Ltd
Profit and Loss Account Year to 31st March 19XX

	£
Sales	8,000,000
Cost of Sales	6,000,000
Gross Profit	2,000,000
Expenses	1,200,000
Operating Profit	800,000
Interest	400,000
Profit before Tax	400,000

Typical Ltd
Balance Sheet Year to 31st March 19XX

	£
Fixed Assets	1,000,000
Current Assets	
Stock	1,000,000
Debtors	900,000
Total	2,900,000
Current Liabilities	
Creditors	900,000
Debt	1,500,000
Capital and Reserves	500,000
Total	2,900,000

The depreciation charge per year is £100,000.

In this company a swing of 25% in the operational cash flow after interest represents £125,000 ((400,000 + 100,000) × 25%). In the real world this would represent a massive increase or decrease in volumes of sales and hence production. If the movement was a fall, it might involve retrenchment and a permanent reduction in the workforce.

Let us take the worst case equivalent example from the working capital cycle. A swing of 25% in each of the components is worth:

Description of Movement	Value
Stocks increase 25%	£250,000
Debtors increase 25%	£225,000
Creditors decrease 25%	£225,000
TOTAL MOVEMENT	£700,000

To compare the two different elements of cash flow for volatility gives the following result. An adverse swing of just 4.5% (value £126,000) in each of the components of the working capital cycle is sufficient in our example to match a swing of 25% (value £125,000) in operating cash flows. All the other elements making up the cash flow of a business are much less volatile.

A swing of 4.5% is easily possible on a month to month basis, and can be equally damaging to cash flow as a 25% reduction in cash generated from operations. Simple errors in purchasing and production can easily push stocks and debtors (through non-payment following disputes over quality or delivery) by 10% to 15% in one month.

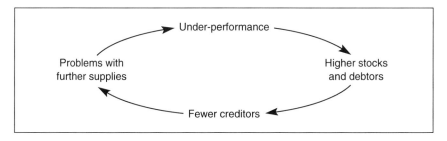

Fig 1.7 The Cash Squeeze

A cash squeeze starting like this can cause creditors to begin withdrawing credit. This further exacerbates the problem such that a vicious circle arises which looks like Fig 1.7.

It follows from this that a fundamental management responsibility in all businesses is to retain tight control of creditors, stocks and debtors at all times.

THE CONSEQUENCES OF HIGH GEARING

What effect does high gearing have on cash flows? Our cash flow model tells us that payments of interest to debt providers represents money leaving the cash flow cycle of the business. Obviously if these values are high relative to a company's ability to generate cash by going around the working capital cycle, there is a constant danger that the lender's appetite for interest and fees will exceed the company's ability to service them. Consequently there is tremendous pressure in highly geared businesses to maintain a consistently high level of performance as any reduction in cash generated can cause a rapid decline into default on the company's debt arrangements.

It follows then that the gearing decision should be taken with a full understanding of the likely volatility of future cash flows. The most recent recession has shown us that some of the buyouts which took place towards the end of the previous boom part of the cycle were unsuitable businesses for a highly leveraged transaction. Examples are furniture manufacturing, construction supply and capital goods businesses. These types of business suffer disproportionately whenever there is a downturn in the economy, losing as much as 50% of their trading volumes. Businesses such as MFI (furniture) and Magnet (building supplies and hardware) both suffered badly.

So to conclude, if a business is vulnerable to changes in general economic conditions this should be taken into account when considering the level of gearing appropriate to the business. In contrast highly leveraged transactions based on food and consumer product businesses tend to be successful as volumes tend to be only minimally affected when economic conditions change.

FORECASTING CASH FLOWS

You will have realised by now that the forecasting of cash flows is a particularly important activity. This is the primary means of anticipating any future shortfall prior to its actual impact on the business. All businesses of any size

should run a rolling twelve month cash flow forecast. Any deterioration lasting more than three months is almost certainly a problem requiring significant and rapid management action to recover performance.

The key to the preparation of an accurate cash flow forecast is to first prepare an accurate and realistic profit and loss account forecast. This provides
us with the data to drive the cash flow forecast, such as sales revenues and
the main expenses. The big unknown in most businesses is the anticipated
level of sales volumes. The sensitivity of gross margin is also important as
purchases and direct labour are usually the largest outflows of cash each
month.

An explanation of the use of spreadsheets to prepare forecasts is beyond
the scope of this book. It is, however, usually the best method of preparation
as it allows easy alteration of any aspect of the forecast. The best test of any
forecast is to compare it with the actual performance each month and amend
it for any major variations, particularly on the expenses side.

There are two pitfalls that are worth mentioning. Computer programs
exist that purport to prepare cash flows and profit and loss accounts in one
combined document. It is not possible conceptually for such a document to
be correct and they can be very misleading. Secondly, it is essential to prepare separate profit and cash flow forecasts for each significant profit centre
within a business. It is important to get down to a reasonable level of detail
as a broad brush approach will not yield meaningful insights as to the cause
of any problems. Whilst a consolidated cash flow summary will reveal the
magnitude of any shortfall of cash in a group it is useless for identifying the
root causes of the problem.

MANAGING CASH FLOWS

Finally, how do we manage to achieve a successful cash flow performance?
The most important thing is foresight. This involves the preparation and
review of realistic and accurate cash flow forecasts for the business.

Secondly, it is important to take early action to attack any deterioration in
cash flows. First determine the cause (internal or external) of any deterioration. If it is internal, take decisive management action to remedy the performance problem. If it is external, develop an appropriate strategic response to
the change in circumstances.

Thirdly, constantly look for ways to enhance cash flows by achieving
improvements in the pattern of receipts and payments. The matrix shown
below summarises the realities of the situation.

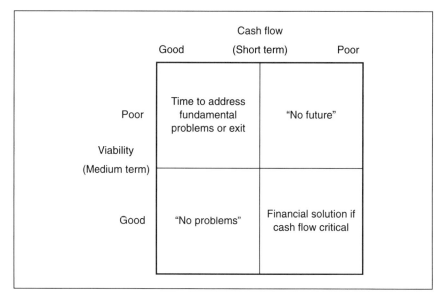

Fig 1.8 Corporate Recovery: What Drives Timescales

SUMMARY

In this chapter we have looked at the constituent parts of a business's cash flows. We have examined the principal strategies available to manage them and introduced the strategic implications of cash flow management, these being the impact of volatility and the behaviour of working capital. In particular we have examined:

- the motivation to trade, and developed this into a simple business cash flow model looking at a trader example;
- the development of a typical cash flow model for manufacturing to illustrate the differing cash flow cycle and implications;
- the complete business model, which was detailed by building in differing terms of trade and the impact on the cash flow;
- a review of 'how we can manage these elements within the cash flow cycle'.

From this base we then examined the assessment of the vulnerability of cash flows depicting four different business profiles and the likely volatility and sensitivity, and finally we reviewed the consequences of high gearing and their impact on cash flow management.

2

CASH FLOW – THE EFFECTS OF BUSINESS RISK

INTRODUCTION

A corporate manager in his assessment of corporate cash flow will inevitably, as part of the overall analysis, need to understand the company's competitive position, its strategy and the resultant business risk effect on cash flow needs.

Every company has a strategy, be it express or implied. Express strategy will normally be well defined and be the result of a structured planning process. Implied strategy on the other hand will be the result of different business units pursuing different (and sometimes conflicting) strategies. The combined result is very often unclear and can cause severe cash flow distortions.

A good starting point in the assessment of corporate risk could be to undertake a general review of how the company's strategy has been formulated.

The Wheel of Competitive Strategy (Fig 2.1) is a device for expressing the main aspects of a company's competitive strategy in summary format. The centre illustrates the corporate objectives and then goes on to state how the corporate is going to compete. The spokes of the wheel are operational factors by which the corporate intends to achieve the 'centre' objectives.

Within each spoke a summarised statement of intent is required.

The designer of this wheel concept states that 'for the corporate to progress effectively, not only must the policies radiate from the centre, but also each of the spokes must link smoothly together.' (See Fig 2.2.)

It is then important to ask: **what considerations are needed in formulating the centre statements for the wheel?**

Fig 2.1 The Wheel of Competitive Strategy

- Device for focussing on key aspects of strategy
- Segments of wheel require statements of operational policy
- Each segment must interlink and reflect centre goals

Fig 2.2

USING SWOT ANALYSIS

The most frequently used model for this is known as a **SWOT analysis.**

SWOT stands for Strengths, Weaknesses, Opportunities and Threats. In carrying out this type of assessment of strengths and weaknesses we are undertaking an internal audit of the corporate. In evaluating opportunities and threats we are carrying out an external review of the market-place in which the corporate is currently operating (see Figs 2.3 and 2.4).

INDUSTRY IDENTIFICATION

As part of this review of the company's individual strategies the manager must analyse in depth the industry within which the company operates to identify its particular characteristics, features and peculiar risk profiles.

The industry structure will have a strong influence in determining the competitive rules of the game – as well as the strategies potentially available to the corporate. Outside forces will usually affect all companies in the industry and therefore another key issue will be the corporate's ability to deal with external factors.

The intensity of competition within the industry will be determined by industry economics as well as the strategies of current competitors. A well known model for looking at industry competition is Porter's Five Forces model (see Fig 2.5). This is a framework for identifying the collective strength or weaknesses of the factors driving industry competition. The intensity of the forces will in turn drive the rates of return on capital employed. For example, in an industry such as tyres, paper or steel there is high intensity of competition and therefore economics dictate a low return on capital employed. Examples of relatively mild intensity could be oil field equipment, cosmetics and toiletries; these types of industries will generate high returns.

Porter's Five Forces model

The five forces to be considered are the external aspects of the bargaining power of buyers, the bargaining power of suppliers, the threat of new entrants and the threat of substitute products or services, and the internal force of competitive rivalry.

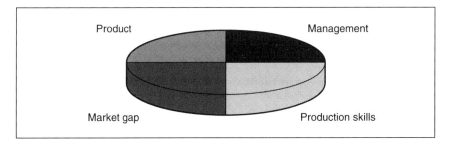

Fig 2.3 SWOT analysis

- your product
- the size of the market
- production capacity
- availability of raw materials
- financial resources
- management expertise

Fig 2.4 SWOT

Knowledge of sources of competitive pressure

This will provide the corporate with the groundwork to develop a strategic action plan. Competitive pressures will highlight the critical strengths and weaknesses of the company and also pinpoint the company position within an industry. Additionally, it will highlight areas which promise to hold the most significance in terms of opportunities and threats to the corporate. The corporate will then need to decide what strategic changes are possible to take advantage of the opportunities or indeed to defend against external threats.

Barriers to entry

Economies of scale tend to deter entrants to the industry by forcing the entrant to come in on a very large scale or to accept a significant cost disadvantage within the industry. Main frame computers provide a useful example. Product differentiation or brand identification can also create a barrier by forcing potential entrants to spend heavily to overcome existing customer loyalty; for example in the sports shoe industry.

Another barrier to entry could be the significant capital investment requirements and advertising programmes needed to carry out an entry programme. This will in turn require significant financial resources together with capital for current asset investment.

The bargaining power of buyers

Buyers will compete within the industry by forcing down prices and trying to bargain for more services of a higher quality. This in turn will lead to more competition within the industry, and all of this is at the expense of industry profitability. The power of the industry's important buying groups

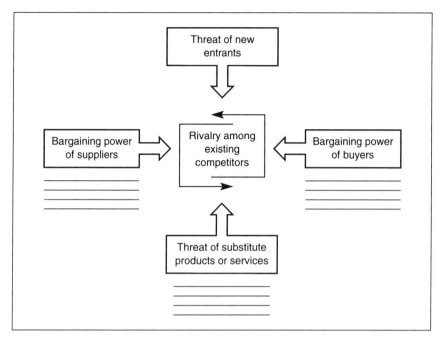

Fig 2.5 Porter's Five Forces Model

will depend on a number of characteristics within the market situation and also on the relative importance of purchases from the industry in the context of the overall business size.

The bargaining power of suppliers

Suppliers can exert power over participants within an industry by threatening to raise prices or reduce the quality of purchased goods and services. Suppliers with great power can squeeze profitability out of an industry which is unable to recover cost increases by adding on to its own prices. An example of this could be chemical companies who have contributed to the erosion of profitability of contract aerosol packaging because the packagers are facing intense competition from self-manufacture by their buyers, and accordingly they have limited freedom to raise their prices.

In conclusion, the use of this type of structural analysis can help identify a large number of factors that can potentially have an impact on industry competition. This is therefore a useful tool to the corporate manager in his assessment of corporate risk and its subsequent effect on cash flow issues.

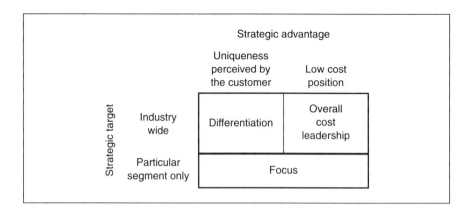

Fig 2.6 Three Generic Strategies

THREE GENERIC STRATEGIES

Depending on a company's positioning with regard to its strategic advantage and also its strategic target, generic strategies tend to fall into three principal types: overall cost leadership, differentiation and focus (see Fig 2.6).

Overall cost leadership

This type of strategy requires a rigorous pursuit of efficiencies in terms of costs and overheads, volume and systems. It is essential that very close managerial attention is given in order to achieve these efficiency aims. Achieving a low cost position will help defend against competitors and businesses will still obtain profitable returns although these may be quite fine. It also provides a defence against buyer power trying to force down prices and generally will give a favourable position from which to defend against low cost substitute products or new entrants to the market. Examples of this include Black and Decker and Amstrad.

Differentiation

This strategy requires the creation of differentiation in terms of the product or service offered by the business. Some examples of design or brand images would be Mercedes or Porsche cars and Caterpillar construction equipment. By adopting a differentiation strategy this should lead in turn to an ability to earn above average returns within an industry. Differentiation should also prove a defence against rivals provided there is customer loyalty to the brand image of the particular corporate.

Focus

This entire strategy is built around servicing a particular target market and all functional policies are developed with this objective in mind. An effective and efficient service to the target will be necessary for success relative to competitors who are generally competing more broadly. A focussed strategy can adopt a low cost position for its strategic target, as shown in the diagram, or aim for differentiation or a combination of both.

CASE STUDY: HI-TEC SPORTS

Background

Hi-Tec was started in the 1970s by Frank Van Wezel. In 1982, following a change of strategy, the company set about creating a new brand name – Hi-Tec. Growth has been very significant and over the period from January 1989 to January 1992 sales increased by 94.2%. Net assets have grown from £19.5 million to £25.4 million over the same period.

SUMMARY

	1992 £'000	1991 £'000	1990 £'000	1989 £'000
Profit and Loss Account				
Turnover	127,826	119,780	83,651	65,818
Operating (loss)/profit before exceptional items	11,574	10,372	7,891	7,826
(Loss)/profit before taxation	9,061	8,233	6,400	7,013
(Loss)/profit attributable to shareholders	5,703	5,146	4,001	4,544
(Loss)/earnings per share	15.7p	14.4p	11.2p	13.4p
Dividends per share	5.5p	5.0p	4.5p	4.5p

	1992 £'000	1991 £'000	1990 £'000	1989 £'000
Net Assets				
Fixed assets	2,475	1,955	937	763
Stocks	33,463	36,166	21,143	17,179
Debtors	29,202	27,016	22,529	16,526
Creditors	(19,578)	(26,567)	(17,168)	(9,086)
Capital employed	45,562	38,570	27,441	25,382
Shareholders' funds	25,247	22,327	20,742	19,441
Minority interests	135	126	92	80
Net assets	25,382	22,453	20,834	19,521
Debt (net of cash)	20,180	16,117	6,607	5,861
Capital employed	45,562	38,570	27,441	25,382
Net assets per share	71p	64p	60p	56p
Gross Profit/Sales	34%	32%	32%	34%

Industry analysis

By utilising the Porter model for industry analysis we can pinpoint the extreme rivalry between competitors in this particular industry and also consider the threat of new entrants, the bargaining power of customers, the bargaining power of suppliers and the threat of substitutes.

Beginning with rivalry amongst existing competitors; as already mentioned earlier this industry is fiercely competitive. The 'big names' are well known brands such as Nike, Reebok, Adidas and Hi-Tec. There are also many other less well known brands and lots of 'unknown' cheaper sports shoes.

Considering next the 'bargaining power of buyers'. This can also be rated as high since although there is brand loyalty, the buyer has a multitude of choice. There is also a very wide range of prices. Demographic changes and fashion trends also impact heavily on buyer patterns as does the influence of large advertising campaigns featuring well known personalities.

The 'bargaining power of suppliers' is a mixed picture. Whilst there are many potential suppliers in South East Asia and China for lesser known or not known shoes, it would be quite difficult for the larger players to switch from their main sources. This is due to large order sizes and long delivery times. Also, considerable capital investment is needed for the special features associated with the leading brands.

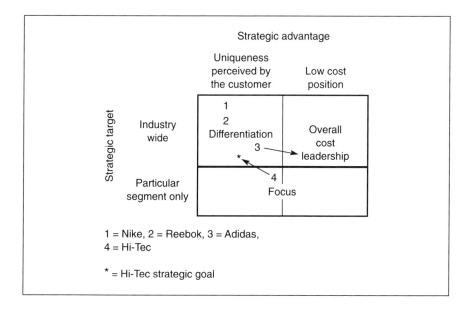

Fig 2.7 Sports Shoe Sector

The threat of new entrants bringing in substitute products is high at the lower price end of the market where the main considerations will be costs, and targeting focussed segments of the market. At the top end of the market it will be much more difficult to penetrate the established brand names and market positioning of the larger players, hence the threat of new entrants attacking the big players will be much lower.

Competitive positioning

Next we can look at a model for generic strategies and try to position some of the well known players in terms of product differentiation and focus (see Fig 2.7).

The diagram illustrates that Nike and Reebok are both brand leaders in perception and have wide target areas, while Adidas is losing ground. Hi-tec's corporate strategy is to develop its products world-wide and at the same time improve the image perception of its brands.

Porter's view is that the most dangerous strategy for a corporate is to become 'stuck in the middle' thereby lacking strategic advantage and directional focus.

Hi-Tec's 1991 mission statement included the following:

'The recent introduction of new ranges of footwear, sports/leisurewear and accessories will further the Group's ambitions to strengthen its international brand portfolio.'

The January 1992 year end results indicated again a successful year, although sales growth slowed to an increase of only seven per cent compared with the previous year's growth of 43%. An operating profit of £11.8 million was recorded compared with £10.4 million in 1991.

The chart below shows a decline in sales within the UK but improvements in all other areas of the world. It is also very significant that the UK provided 75% of profits in 1991 and despite the decline in 1992 still provided 59.5%.

SEGMENT INFORMATION

	1992			1991		
	Turnover £'000	Profit £'000	Net Assets £'000	Turnover £'000	Profit £'000	Net Assets £'000
Graphical Area						
UK	60,631	6,883	17,277	70,627	7,780	10,800
Continental Europe	33,063	1,778	11,787	23,538	936	11,903
North America	22,645	1,932	10,349	15,880	1,266	7,994
Rest of World	11,487	981	6,149	9,735	390	7,873
	127,826			119,780		
Operating Profit		11,574			10,372	

Cash flow

Within the 1992 financial statements cash flow was shown in the new reporting format as per the 'Financial Reporting Standard' (FRS 1) which came into effect in March 1992.

CONSOLIDATED CASH FLOW STATEMENT

		1992	1991
For the year ended 2 February 1992	Note	£'000	£'000
Net cash inflow from operating activities	25	**7,538**	(894)
Returns on investments and servicing of finance			
Interest received		**178**	80
Interest paid		**(2,691)**	(2,219)
Dividends paid		**(1,834)**	(1,569)
Net cash outflow from returns on investment and servicing of finance		**(4,347)**	(3,708)
		3,191	(4,602)
Taxation			
UK and overseas corporate tax paid		**(5,294)**	(1,856)
Investing activities			
Purchase of subsidiaries		**(1,677)**	(1,431)
Tangible fixed assets acquired		**(1,147)**	(1,508)
Tangible fixed assets sold		**78**	17
Intangible fixed assets acquired		**(75)**	(13)
Net cash flow before financing		**(4,924)**	(9,510)
Financing			
Issue of ordinary share capital		**(861)**	–
Proceeds of long-term borrowings		**(3,037)**	–
Net cash flow from financing		**(3,898)**	–
Decrease in cash and cash equivalents		**(1,026)**	(9,510)
		(4,924)	(9,510)

RECONCILIATION OF OPERATING PROFIT TO NET
CASH INFLOW FROM OPERATING ACTIVITIES

	1992 £'000	1991 £'000
Operating profit	11,574	10,372
Depreciation charges	726	515
Profit/Loss on sale of tangible fixed assets	(18)	33
Stocks	2,703	(15,023)
Debtors	(2,043)	(5,054)
Creditors	(5,619)	8,592
Exchange	214	(340)
Other	1	11
Net cash inflow from operating activities	7,538	(894)

I am sure readers will agree that this new cash flow format is a great improvement over the previous source and application of funds layout which tended to confuse rather than clarify the key cash flow movements. The cash flow document shows that in 1991 Hi-Tec's net cash inflow from operations was negative £894,000 after heavy cash investments in stocks and debtors (£15 million and £5 million) with some sourcing to offset this from creditors of £8.5 million. The cash flow was therefore negative before payments of interest, dividend, taxation, subsidiaries and fixed asset expenditure. The 'bottom line' position was very negative at £9.5 million and this must be counterbalanced as illustrated in the financing section.

The 1992 cash flow shows the de-stocking position and reduction in creditors to give a resulting net positive cash flow from operations of £7.5 million. Following the statement through, after payment of interest and dividends the cash flow was still positive – £3.2 million. However after payment of tax, subsidiaries and fixed assets, the net cash flow was again negative at £4.9 million requiring further financing.

The 1992 accounts also mentioned a 'rights issue'. This rights issue, which raised £10.3 million net of expenses, received strong support from existing and new shareholders with a take-up of 98.6% of the shares issued. The proceeds reduced the year-end gearing as at 2 February 1992 on a pro-forma basis to approximately 29%, with net borrowings (after receipt of the rights issue proceeds) reduced to £9.9 million.

The company took the opportunity of the rights issue to create a wider market in the company's shares. Members of the family did not take up rights, with the result that they now hold some 56% of the ordinary share capital and, following the placing of our entitlements, a number of new shareholders have been introduced to the company.

Details of the subsequent competitive attack in 1993 and depressed state of the economy were well illustrated in the following extracts.

The Times 25 May 1993

HI-TEC SPORTS MISSES ITS STEPS

Depressed consumer spending, a savage price war in the UK and poor trading in Europe combined to push Hi-tec Sports, the sports shoe and leisurewear group, to a pre-tax loss of £8.3 million in the year to the end of January, compared with profit of £9.06 million last year.

Losses were exacerbated by a £4.82 million exceptional charge, due to restructuring costs for closing down a string of European subsidiaries.

Group turnover fell 16 per cent to £106.9 million, with UK sales down 38 per cent and those in continental Europe 15 per cent lower. However, North American sales jumped 30 per cent.

Hi-tec maintained its market share in the UK, retaining a number one position in volume terms. However, this was achieved at the expense of profit margins. The UK businesses suffered an operating loss of £1.6 million (£6.9 million profit).

Europe dived to an operating loss of £2.7 million (£1.8 million profit) and is still proving to be a difficult market, but the closure of European subsidiaries should reduce the fixed cost base by £2.5 million annually. North America was a bright spot, with operating profits ahead 24 per cent to £2.4 million, boosted by strong sales of rugged footwear for the fast growing hiking market.

Losses per share amounted to 18.8p, against earnings of 16.1p a share last time. The total dividend is cut to 2p (5.5p), with a reduced final payout of 1p (3.85p).

Extract from 1993 Hi-Tec Annual Accounts

CHAIRMAN'S STATEMENT

As I indicated in April, the last year has been the most difficult in your Company's history. The long, deep recession in the UK, coupled with economic deterioration in Europe, caused a sharp reversal in Hi-Tec's fortunes, leading in turn to our first ever loss at the interim stage.

Although there was some improvement in the second half of the year, when a small operating profit was achieved, the results for the year as a whole are disappointing. For the year ended 31 January 1993, Hi-Tec made a post interest trading loss of £3.5m before taking account of exceptional restructuring costs of £4.8m in respect of the European businesses, giving rise to a loss before tax of £8.3m (1992: profit before tax of £9.1m). After a small tax credit this translates into a loss after tax of £8.1m (1992: profit £5.7m). The loss per share was 18.8p (1992: earnings 16.1).

Group turnover declined by 16% to £106.9m, with UK sales falling by 38% and those in Continental Europe by 15%. However, these sharp reductions were partially offset by a 30% increase in North American sales and a 3% increase elsewhere in the world.

Review of Operations

United Kingdom
The UK business, despite being hit by recession and a harmful price war, retained its market position by volume but produced an operating loss of £1.6m (1992: £6.9m operating profit). In response, the Group reduced its workforce in this country by 20% and liquidated surplus warehouse stocks. Both actions are designed to return operations in the UK to profitability.

Continental Europe
In Europe, our Bad Boys business continued to trade profitably but the network of European subsidiaries serving the Hi-Tec range lost money, producing an overall operating loss in Europe of £2.7m (1992: £1.8m operating profit). Your board took the view that it was not appropriate to just sit out the European recession and await better times. Urgent surgery was required and we are implementing a major restructuring of Hi-Tec's operations in Continental Europe, designed both to reduce significantly the cost structure and maintain market position. The Group's subsidiaries in France, Belgium, Germany, Holland, Switzerland, Denmark and Sweden are being closed, thereby reducing the fixed cost base by some £2.5m annually. Customers in these countries will now be serviced by distributors with back-up from our UK headquarters.

These changes do not affect our Bad Boys range which will continue to operate through the separately managed Cofex Group of companies.

North America and Rest of the World

Hi-Tec's operations in North America increased their operating profits by 24%. In the rest of the world profits fell to £0.4m from £1.0m.

In the US, Hi-Tec specialises in high quality rugged outdoor footwear and is widely recognised as one of the leading pioneers in this fast growing market. The US division now sells over 60 styles of outdoor footwear through more than 2,500 retail footwear accounts throughout the US and Mexico and the last four years has achieved a 37% compound annual growth rate in sales, which have grown from some $13m in 1988 to $44m in the year to January 1993. In 1992, Hi-Tec ranked 17th by sales in the $6 billion US branded athletic footwear market.

We believe that the American product range has considerable potential elsewhere in the world and a comprehensive rugged outdoor range is now being actively marketed in both the UK and Europe. We expect to develop further the American company and its product range.

Product Development and Marketing

The Group continues to improve its product range of quality high technology athletic footwear, actively endorsed by leading sportsmen and women in each field.

Hi-Tec, as a leading British brand was fittingly nominated by the All England Lawn Tennis Club as the official supplier of footwear to the Championships, Wimbledon.

A compact Wimbledon collection consisting of four quality models has subsequently been developed featuring the ABC Wimbledon Professional which incorporates Hi-Tec's unique world patented Airball concept that offers essential injury-preventing shock absorption. Wimbledon models will not only be worn by all ball boys and girls at Wimbledon but also by flamboyant Frenchman Henri Leconte during his 1993/94 playing schedule.

As the world's largest supplier of squash shoes we have also made important technological advances with the launch of the Hi-Tec Adrenalin, a shoe which was developed in close conjunction with six of the world's best professionals including World No. 1 Jansher Khan. The Hi-Tec Squash Adrenalin was officially previewed at the prestigious eighth Hi-Tec British Open Squash Tournament in April and will be in-store from September.

In trying times the strength of a Company depends on the abilities and commitment of its staff.

On behalf of the board and shareholders, I would like to thank everyone who has worked in our organisation wherever they may be located. It has been a superb example of teamwork at its best.

Dividends

The Directors are recommending a final dividend of 0.1p net per ordinary share to give a full year dividend of 2.0p (1992: 5.5p), reflecting their confidence in the future trading of the Group, despite the difficulties of the last year. If approved at the Annual General Meeting on 15 July, the dividend will be paid on 30 July to shareholders on the register at the close of business on 17 June. Shareholders will again be offered the opportunity to receive their dividend entitlement by way of additional shares rather than cash; the Directors have undertaken to do this in respect of their own entitlement.

Current Trading

Results from our operations since the year end continue to show an encouraging trend and we anticipate the Group returning to profitability during the current year. In the UK market, where conditions proved to be so difficult last year, prices are firming as the retailing climate improves and our UK operations made a small operating profit in the first quarter.

Our US operations continue to do well and our restructuring in Europe is expected to ensure significant cost savings in the current year. The performance of Bad Boys is, however, expected to be affected by recessionary conditions in Europe.

We are fully committed to restoring the fortunes of the Group and are confident that the radical actions we have taken will produce encouraging results in due course.

SUMMARY

	1993 £'000	1992 £'000
Profit and Loss Account		
Turnover	106,896	127,826
Operating (loss)/profit before exceptional items	(1,475)	11,574
(Loss)/profit before taxation	(8,301)	9,061
(Loss)/profit attributable to shareholders	(8,108)	5,703
(Loss)/earnings per share	(18.8p)	15.7p
Dividends per share	2.0p	5.5p
Net Assets		
Fixed assets	3,138	2,475
Stocks	32,614	33,463

Debtors	**30,920**	29,202
Creditors	**(20,360)**	(19,578)
Capital employed	**46,312**	45,562
Shareholders' funds	**25,378**	25,247
Minority interests	**183**	135
Net assets	**25,561**	25,382
Debt (net of cash)	**20,751**	20,180
Capital employed	**46,312**	45,562
Net assets per share	**55p**	71p
Gross Profit/Sales	**31%**	34%

The table above illustrates the sales decline between 1992 and 1993 in summary format. It is also significant that competitive pressure, primarily from Nike and Reebok within the UK market-place, forced the gross profit margin down to 31% compared with the previous year's figure of 34%. This erosion of margin together with the sales decline led to a reduced level of contribution that was insufficient to cover selling, distribution and administrative expenses. Hence an operating loss of £1.5 million was incurred before exceptional items.

Segment Information

SEGMENT INFORMATION

	1993			1992		
	Turnover £'000	**(Loss)/ Profit £'000**	**Net Assets £'000**	Turnover £'000	Profit £'000	Net Assets £'000
Graphical Area						
UK	**37,485** (35%)	**(1,577)**	**12,936**	60,631 (47.4%)	6,883	17,277
Continental Europe	**28,190**	**(2,712)**	**10,521**	33,063	1,778	11,787

North America	**29,387**	**2,399**	**17,463**	22,645	1,932	10,349
Rest of World	**11,834**	**415**	**5,393**	11,487	981	6,149
	106,896			127,826		
Operating (loss)/profit		(1,475)			11,574	

This chart shows the decline in sales both in the UK and Continental Europe. The UK sales percentage has fallen again and now represents only 35% of total turnover. The resultant swing from an operating profit of £11.6 million to an operating loss of £1.5 million is also illustrated and further sub-analysed.

The impact on cash flow

The operating loss of £1.5 million plus the exceptional restructuring costs of £4.8 million mentioned in the Chairman's statement led to an opening operating negative cash flow after exceptional items of £6.29 million as compared with a positive cash flow of £11.57 million in 1992 – as shown below.

RECONCILIATION OF OPERATING PROFIT TO NET CASH INFLOW FROM OPERATING ACTIVITIES

	1993 £'000	1992 £'000
Operating (loss)/profit after exceptional items	**(6,295)**	11,574
Depreciation charges	**882**	726
Loss/(profit) on sale of tangible fixed assets	**11**	(18)
Stocks	**849**	2,703
Creditors	**(573)**	(2,043)
Foreign exchange movement	**5,592**	(5,619)
Other	**437**	214
Net cash inflow from operating activities	**903**	7,538

Close examination reveals that after sourcing additional creditors of £5.6 million the net cash inflow from operations was just under £1 million positive despite the negative cash flow opening of £6.3 million.

CONSOLIDATED CASH FLOW STATEMENT

	1993 £'000	1992 £'000
For the year ended 31 January 1993		
Net cash inflow from operating activities	**903**	**7,538**
Returns on investment and servicing of finance		
Interest receivable	**136**	178
Interest paid	**(2,142)**	(2,691)
Dividends	**(1,843)**	(1,843)
Net cash outflow from returns on investment		
and servicing of finance	**(3,849)**	(4,347)
Sub Total	**(2,946)**	3,191
Taxation		
UK and overseas corporate tax paid	**(4,268)**	(5,294)
Investing activities		
Purchase of subsidiaries	**(4,399)**	(1,677)
Issue of shares to minority	**10**	–
Tangible fixed assets acquired	**(1,181)**	(1,147)
Tangible fixed assets sold	**38**	78
Intangible fixed assets acquired	**(202)**	(75)
Net cash outflow before financing	**(12,948)**	**(4,924)**
Financing		
Issue of ordinary share capital	**(11,436)**	(861)
Capital to be issued	**(941)**	–
Proceeds of long-term borrowings	**(66)**	(3,037)
Net cash outflow from financing	**(12,443)**	(3,898)
Decrease in cash and cash equivalents	**(505)**	(1,026)
	(12,948)	(4,924)

The table above gives us the continuation of the cash flow picture showing cash flow becoming negative by £2.9 million after payment of interest charges and dividends. Other key figures are also shown and you can see that after all payments were made, the Net Cash Outflow before financing was £12.9 million negative.

It can be seen that a huge increase (approximately £8 million) occurred in negative cash flow. This is counterbalanced by financing, primarily through the share issue mentioned previously.

I am sure we will all be watching with interest for the 1994 Hi-Tec results. The case clearly illustrates the effect of competition and recession on cash flow and also the usefulness of the new FRS1 cash flow statement documents in focussing more clearly on the company's cash movements.

IN CONCLUSION

The purpose of this second chapter has been to create an awareness of business risk and its impact on cash flow requirements. A good corporate manager must be able to analyse, identify and understand the company's specific strategy and the competition within the market-place in order to determine the likely cash flow needs and the appropriate financial structure and products to meet those needs. In particular we have examined:

- the starting point for the formulation of strategy using the 'Wheel of competitive strategy', developing this to understand how the business is going to compete;
- SWOT analysis as a tool to help undertake a corporate audit of resources and external factors;
- next we undertook an industry analysis using Porter's Five Forces model; developing this to examine generic strategies of cost leadership, differentiation and focus;
- we then introduced the Hi-Tec Sports case study in order to consider and develop the impact of the effects of business risk on the future cash flows of Hi-Tec, introducing the new cash flow statement format (FRS1).

3

CASH FLOW – SQUEEZING OUT MORE CASH

INTRODUCTION

Cash flow does not mean profits. For example, poor or declining profitability will not necessarily result in weak cash flows. If a company sells very little over the course of a year, it may still generate significant amounts of cash by selling off plant and equipment. If it uses up finished stocks and does not invest in more raw material, then it may conserve cash whereas another company with the same profit margin will not conserve cash if it has been investing in replacement of or increases in stock levels. Corporate managers should be more interested in cash flow than 'profit'. Published profit can be easily manipulated whereas the true cash generated by a company cannot.

What is meant by cash flow and what is its significance? It can be defined in many ways, but whatever the terminology, the basic item is gross operating cash flow. This is the amount of cash generated from a company's sales after cost of goods sold and other operating costs are deducted. From this must be deducted (or added) the cash spent on movements in working investment (debtors, stocks and creditors being the principal elements). The resultant cash generated from operations is usually called **net operating cash flow (NOCF).**

Why is NOCF significant? Because we are concerned with the ability of a company to generate enough cash from its ongoing business to cover its financing needs (ie interest payments, principal payments on long term debt and dividend payments). There are other needs which will be examined later, but lenders and bankers extending credit are primarily interested in the capacity of existing or prospective clients to meet their financial obligations from within their own resources, whether these obligations be loans or contingent liabilities.

Few credit committees will accept refinancing from other banks as the proposed source of repayment of outstanding debt. Clearly, repayment may only be sought when a borrower is ailing and may have breached the terms of its loan agreement: in these circumstances other banks will rarely be willing to provide refinancing. While there may be assets available for liquidation, these would not necessarily be very saleable. The company may have gone out of business precisely because its products were unsaleable.

Furthermore in a publicised 'fire-sale' potential purchasers are well aware that a bank is not interested in owning and maintaining assets such as a crane or hotel. Prices offered therefore will generally be well below book value as banks seek to move items off their own balance sheets and prevent further waste of management time.

Net operating cash flow, or NOCF, is a key indicator that a company has the capacity to meet its main obligations. A company's record of generating cash from operations is instructive in itself for it can be used as a base for estimating future capacity.

Where do we find the necessary information to be able to construct a cash flow analysis? The prime source is usually a company's annual accounts. It is vital therefore to be able to read accounts in a meaningful way and to be able to extract the information required in order to construct a cash flow analysis. The basic elements of this are beginning and ending balance sheets, the profit and loss statement and the notes to the accounts.

Under the terms of FRS 1 (Financial Reporting Standard 1) companies must now provide a standard format for their cash flows, and include this in their annual reports with the profit and loss statement and balance sheets. The major categories covered are cash from operating activities, inflows and outflows on investments and the servicing of finance, taxation, investment in and disposal of assets and movements regarding financing. Whilst this arrangement is a considerable improvement over the funds flow statement which it supersedes there is still a need for the analyst to construct his own statement in order to distinguish between true cash movements and non-cash balance sheet changes.

Since the purpose of the analysis is to measure a company's capacity to meet its financial obligations from within its own resources, net operating cash flow must be regarded as the most critical source of cash, being the return from the ongoing, underlying business. Although cash may be generated from other sources, these cannot be relied upon as continuing sources. A company, for example, may be able to sell off assets one year, but obviously this process cannot be indefinite as there will be insufficient assets to continue the business. The focus of analysis is therefore not only sources of funds, but in particular **operating** sources of cash.

How is 'cash generated from operations' calculated? A simple example might be as follows:

Sales	100
Less: Cost of goods sold	(75)
Less: Admin and costs selling	(10)
= Gross Operating Cash Flow (GOCF)	**15**

Note: The GOCF number is equal to net income and depreciation and non-cash charges.

WORKING INVESTMENT	
Purchase Stocks	(5)
Increase Debtors	(5)
Increase Creditors	5
Movement in Working Investment (WI)	(5)
= Net Operating Cash Flow (NOCF)	**10**
USES	
Capital Expenditure	(15)
Dividend	(5)
Debt Repayment	(5)
= Net Funds After Uses	**(15)**
SOURCES	
Equity	5
Bank Loan	5
= Net Movement in Cash	**(5)**

Gross operating cash flow has been arrived at by taking sales less cost of goods sold and other profit and loss cash charges. You can reach the same figure by adding net income, depreciation and non-cash charges. This is perfectly acceptable provided that the analyst understands that this is a short cut.

OPERATING CASH FLOW AND THE MARGIN OF SAFETY

Introduction

The ability to quickly pinpoint the margin of safety in any business is a very useful tool in terms of operational cash flow planning. If we see a business with a good margin of safety then there will be comfort in knowing that positive cash flow can still be generated even with a given fall-back of performance in terms of sales output and profit revenue.

Definition

The margin of safety is the drop in sales that can be carried before a loss occurs. This figure is usually calculated as a percentage of sales.

Calculations can be made both mathematically and graphically. Before we can begin calculations, let us set some guidelines to help with the analysis.

Analysing costs

The total cost of selling a product or service does not vary directly with volume! The reason for this is that some costs are volume orientated (e.g. materials) while others tend to be constant or fixed over a period (e.g. rent and depreciation). If we take an example:

PROFIT BUDGET SUMMARISED

	£000	£
Sales		120,000
Less purchases		72,000
Gross profit		48,000
Less overheads		
Wages	12,000	
Advertising	2,000	
Rent/rates	9,500	
Light/heat/water	1,300	
Insurance	750	
Repairs/renewals	960	
Motor expenses	840	
Telephone	650	
Sundries	1,200	
Accountant's charges	1,350	
Depreciation	1,625	32,175
Net profit before tax		15,825

From this we can see that the volume related costs in this case are our purchases of goods for re-sale and all the remaining costs can be classified as fixed.

Variable and fixed costs

- the *variable costs* are volume orientated
- the *fixed costs* are more static over a period of time

Now we can alter the format of our budget as follows:

	£000
Sales	120,000
Less variable costs	72,000
Contribution	48,000
Less fixed costs	32,175
Net profit	15,825

Contribution

The contribution is the difference between the selling price and variable costs (the direct costs of the sale). The relationship between contribution and sale price is known as the contribution ratio. In our example:

$$\frac{48,000}{12,0000} = .40$$

This ratio is frequently referred to as the profit-volume, or PV ratio. In our example every additional £100 of sales will generate £40 additional contribution to overheads and profitability.

The break-even sales point

The break-even point of a business is the point at which the business is making neither profit nor loss. It is the point at which the contributions earned from *sales* equal the fixed costs.

A basic formula for calculating break-even sales is

$$BE = \frac{\text{fixed costs}}{\text{pv ratio}}$$

In our example therefore

$$BE = \frac{£32175000}{.40}$$

$$= £8043800$$

To check that calculation:

Sales budgeted	£120,000,000
Break-even sales	80,438,000
Profit producing sales	39,562,000
@ contribution	
Gives net profit	£15,825,000

(@ contribution 0.40)

Graphic presentation

Presenting information graphically helps to clarify the differing break-even profiles that can be seen within corporates, as Figure 3.1 shows.

We begin then by setting the graph's axes as follows:

vertical axis   = £ sales/costs
horizontal axis = percentage output

The graph shows us the break-even point. This is the point where the sales line crosses our total cost line: the point in business where we make neither profit nor loss.

The graph also shows a net profit measurement between sales and total costs. If you take a ruler and extend a line horizontally from the break-even point to the vertical sales/costs axis – you will confirm the break-even point at £30 000 of sales.

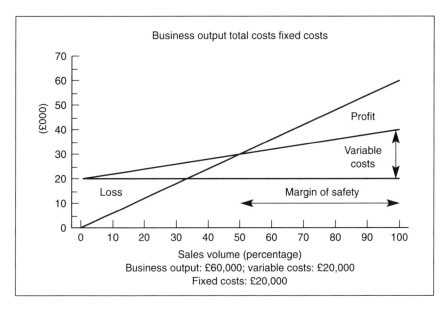

Fig 3.1 Break-even Analysis

Margin of safety calculation

Now that we understand the positioning of the break-even point we can move on to our calculation of the margin of safety. This aspect is very important to us in understanding the business profile in terms of the cash flow fall-back positions that could be encountered.

As stated earlier the margin of safety is the drop in sales that can be carried before a loss occurs. This figure is usually calculated as a percentage of sales.

The calculation mathematically therefore is:

$$\text{MOS} = \frac{\text{Expected Sales} - \text{Break-even Sales}}{\text{Expected Sales}} \times 100$$

An example

Returning to our example

Sales	£120,000,000
Variable costs	£72,000,000
Contribution (pv ratio .40)	£48,000,000
Fixed cost	£32,175,000
Net profit	£15,825,000

The break-even was calculated at £80,438,000. Therefore the margin of safety is:

$$= \frac{S - BE}{S} \times 100$$

$$= \frac{120,000 - 80,438}{120,000} \times 100$$

$$= 1/3 \qquad \times 100$$

$$= 33.1/3\%$$

We are saying therefore that sales could drop in this example by $33\frac{1}{3}\%$ before break-even will occur. That is obviously a reasonable margin of safety and gives a good fall-back in terms of operational cash flow.

Another example

Examine the two contrasting profiles of companies A and B shown in Fig 3.2.

Differing profiles in terms of cost structures will give us differing sensitivities to cash fall-back positions. Figure 3.2 shows companies A and B both giving the same net return on sales but having a different cost structure.

The pv ratios are very different, and you can see what happens in the case of a 20% reduction in sales volume (Fig 3.3).

Company A is most sensitive to sales volume reductions because of its high fixed cost structure and swings into loss and therefore negative operating cash flow!!

	£000 Co. A	£000 Co. B
Sales	300.00	500.00
Variable costs	80.00	375.00
Contribution	220.00	125.00
Fixed costs	190.00	75.00
Net profit	30.00	50.00
Return on sales (%)	10.00	10.00
P.V. ratio	0.73	0.25

Fig 3.2 Exercise: Companies A & B

	£000 Co. A	£000 Co. B
New sales	240	400
New variable costs	64	300
Contribution	176	100
Fixed costs	190	75
Net profit	−14	25

Fig 3.3 20% Reduction in Sales

WORKING INVESTMENT AND BUSINESS CYCLES

Cash flow is essentially uncertain in that it is based initially on the projections of future operating income. This can be influenced by a number of factors, including:

- technological problems or breakthrough;
- substitute products developed by competitors or new products by the company;
- product cannot satisfy regulatory requirements, or a regulatory breakthrough is made;
- economic recession or boom.

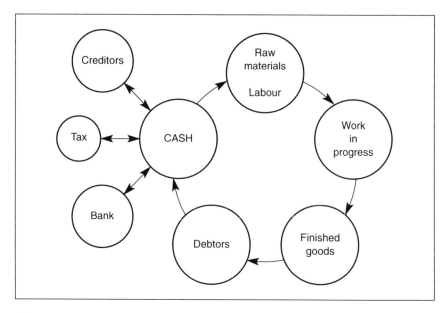

Fig 3.4 Liquidity: the Working Capital Cycle

As stated in Chapter one, the business cycle results from the nature of a company's product and the factors and risks involved in creating and selling the product. To understand business cycles in more detail we therefore need to understand the process through which companies create and use cash.

A manufacturing company's normal operating activity can be described as follows. Cash is used to buy raw materials; this action creates accounts payable; labour costs and overheads are added to provide goods for resale. Goods are then sold normally giving rise to debtors on credit terms. These accounts are settled and the business ends up with cash again – hopefully more than at the beginning of the cycle.

Why is it important to understand the business cycle?

- to develop an understanding of the cash flow risks that businesses are exposed to at different stages of the operating process;
- to understand the process by which businesses consume and generate cash at the operating level;
- to gain an appreciation of the financing needs of a business, and to evaluate if financing is structured appropriately for that business;

- to gain an appreciation of the investment requirements of a business and to evaluate if investment decisions are appropriate for that business.

RISKS INHERENT IN THE BUSINESS CYCLE

The risk inherent in a company with a long operating cycle is greater than one with a short cycle. The longer the period between the purchase of raw materials and the collection of cash from the buyer of finished goods, the more time there is for things to go wrong.

Additionally, a long cycle usually implies:

- more investment in fixed assets;
- more finance required (debt and equity);
- greater value added so higher risk associated with, for example, labour;
- higher return demanded by shareholders to compensate for higher risk, therefore a need for higher margins.

The reverse is true for a short cycle, as seen in commodity traders who have high turnover, little capital, minimal value added and narrow profit margins.

Business cycles will vary from one industry to another and amongst firms in the same industry. Food processors and grocery retailers are frequently given as examples of industries with lower working investment risks whereas cyclical manufacturing industries, such as steel, are regarded as having especially high working investment risk.

Cash generation in the business cycle

We need to begin by considering what problems are likely at each stage of the cycle:

- the purchase of raw materials (supply, quality)
- the processing/production process (labour, fixed asset investment)
- the sale of finished goods (marketability of goods)
- the collection of receivables (quality of debtors, efficiency of collection)

We stated earlier that the reason for being in business is to generate more cash at the end of the cycle than there was at the beginning through the added value of producing a product for which there is a market demand. However, if prices of inputs, costs and finished goods change then this cycle can become loss-making. If a company manages the cycle inefficiently by

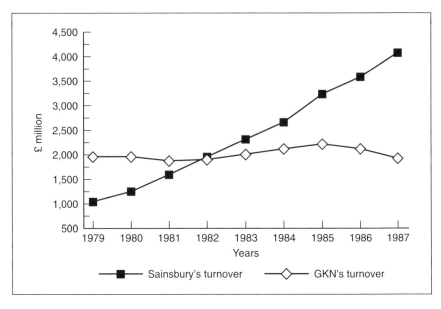

Fig 3.5 Sainsbury's & GKN's Turnover

holding raw materials for long periods of time, allowing long payment periods from debtors but paying creditors more quickly than necessary then the
cycle may also become loss-making (known as negative operating cash
flow). Other situations in which negative operating cash flow can arise
include a company which is growing very quickly and therefore investing
large amounts of cash in stocks and debtors in order to meet large orders. By
contrast declining companies, or companies in recession, can often 'throw
off' cash as a result of running down existing stock and not purchasing new
stock to replace it.

 The challenge for all managers of companies is to run the cycle as quickly
as possible on a continuing basis.

Reviewing variables:

A more in-depth understanding of a company's business risk can be gained
by researching each of the following:

- **Demand variability:** the more stable the demand for a company's products, other things held constant, the lower the company's cash flow risk.

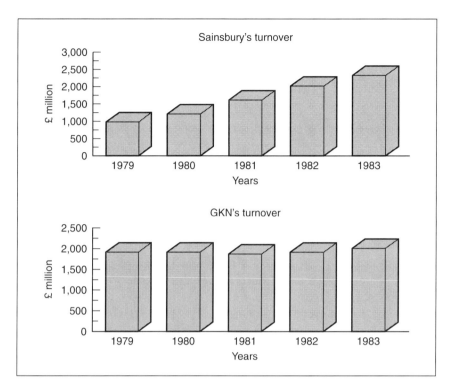

Fig 3.6 Sainsbury's & GKN's Turnover

- **Sales price variability:** companies whose products are sold in highly volatile markets are exposed to more cash flow risk than similar companies whose output prices are relatively stable.
- **Input price variability:** companies whose inputs are highly uncertain are exposed to a high degree of business risk.
- **Ability to adjust output prices for changes in input prices:** some companies have little difficulty in raising their own output prices when input costs rise, and the greater the ability to adjust output prices, the lower the degree of cash flow risk. This factor is especially important during periods of high inflation.
- **The extent to which costs are fixed (operating leverage):** if a high percentage of a company's costs are fixed and hence do not decline when demand falls off, this increases the company's cash flow risk. This factor is called **operating leverage**, and it is discussed earlier in the section on margin of safety.

1983	£M
Sales	2293
+ Stock	142
+ Debtors	17
+ Cash	
(2293/365*2)	13
– Creditors	(251)
(79)/2293*100 =	(79) w/c (3.4%)

Fig 3.7 Sainsbury's Working Capital

Whilst each of these factors is determined largely by the company's industry characteristics, each is also controllable to some extent by management. For example, most companies can, through their marketing policies, take actions to stabilise both unit sales and sales prices. This stabilisation may, however, require either large expenditure on advertising or price concessions to induce customers to commit to purchasing fixed quantities at fixed prices in the future. Similarly, firms can reduce the volatility of future input costs by negotiating long-term labour and materials supply contracts, but they may have to agree to pay prices above the current price level to obtain these contracts.

The relationships between suppliers, buyers and competitors will therefore shape a company's terms of trade – i.e. how quickly it pays suppliers, collects cash from customers and turns its raw materials into finished goods. This can be examined much more closely by looking at the following comparisons of working investment or as it is often termed – Net Working Assets:

CONTRASTING CASH FLOW PROFILES

The finance requirement in the cash conversion cycle is known as the NET WORKING ASSETS (NWA). The amount of Net Working Assets is calculated as follows:

NWA = (Trade Debtors + Stock) – (Trade Creditors)

	£M 1979	
1983		
Sales	1961	1975
Stock	518	403
+		
Net debtors/creditors	28	(52)
Work. cap. requirement	546	351
546/1961 * 100	28%	18%

Fig 3.8 GKN's Working Capital

The period contrasted in Figs 3.5 and 3.6 for Sainsbury and GKN is between 1979 and 1983, encompassing the last recession. Sainsbury's turnover can be seen to be steadily advancing whilst that of GKN is flat, and in fact if inflation is deducted, then the turnover was actually in decline.

Calculating Sainsbury's NWA requirement in 1983 (see Fig 3.7) actually shows a negative, and in fact they are cash generators to the extent of £3.40 for every £100 of sales taking place within the stores. No wonder they are able to embark on new super store developments!

On the other side, as you would expect from a manufacturer, GKN have a positive NWA requirement in 1979 of £28 for every £100 of sales (see Fig 3.8). They are a cash consumer in terms of the NWA cycle. However, by taking very positive action and focussing on their cash management, they were able by 1983 to reduce this burden to 18% – a very significant saving when you consider their large turnover figure.

If we consider this quote from GKN's 1983 Report and Accounts:

'Working capital has remained under close control and improved for the fifth successive year. In spite of capital expenditure of some £28 million higher, there was a net cash inflow in the year of £8.5 million.'

Fig 3.9 shows comparatives in days of NWA cycle.

NWA SURVEY DATA – 450 COMPANIES

Figure 3.10 is based on a survey in conjunction with Manchester Business School and represents stock, debtor, creditor days over a random sample of 450 UK companies. NWA is then calculated and grouped by business type.

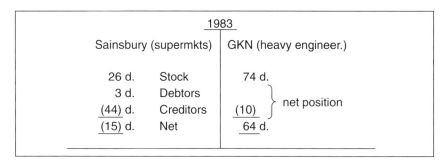

Fig 3.9 Comparison of NWA Cycle in Days

This figure gives an indication **only** of the likely contrasting levels of NWA, this time in terms of the days within the cycle, between differing sectors. The survey was a random sample in terms of size of company and geographical location. It is important to note that the sample was specifically UK based. As you would expect to see, food retailing comes out the lowest at 5 days NWA, and contractors and construction the highest at 138 days, due to the length of the stock periods.

	Debtors	Stock	Creditors	NWA (days)
Industry:–				
Dept. stores	29	54	40	43
Textiles	80	85	72	93
Leisure	88	54	109	33
Food retailing	26	25	46	5
Contractors & Constr.	56	160	78	138
Mechan. engineering	95	64	81	78
Aerospace	88	80	84	84
Household appliances	77	58	69	66
Publishing & print.	102	55	81	76

Fig 3.10 Performance Comparison

A thorough understanding of cash conversion cycles is essential since the cash from the operating cycle will be the 'driver' for all of a company's investment and financing activities.

An understanding of business risk and the business cycle will help the corporate manager to evaluate the long term investment decisions which a company makes (e.g. a new factory, production unit or the acquisition of another company). The forecast operating cash flow following the investment must be sufficient to service any financing associated with this investment, be it long term debt on which interest must be paid or equity on which investors' expectations must be met in terms of dividend payment and capital growth.

So far we have examined cash flow generated from operations and then the absorption or generation of cash within the working investment. Next we will look at the important area of capital expenditure and in particular how we can evaluate a proposed investment.

CAPITAL EXPENDITURE: INTRODUCTION TO METHODS OF APPRAISAL

There are four main methods of appraisal. They have in common a concern with cash flows and all therefore require an evaluation of the initial cost, the running expenses, the estimated life of the project, and the income over the life of the project. Only cash items are included in the calculation of these factors. This means that depreciation is ignored, but the expected residual value of the item in the market-place is included. Taxation, which may be a cash inflow or outflow, can have a significant effect on an investment decision and should always be included. The four methods are payback, average rate of return, net present value, and yield – or internal rate of return.

Payback

This method calculates the time for cash inflows to recoup the initial investment on the project. The payback period indicates to management the time that the investment is at risk: the shorter the length of the period to payback the better.

This method is widely used because it is simple to understand. It provides a clear indication of the time required to convert a 'risky' investment into a safe one. It does not, however, pay any heed to several factors: the timing of cash flows, the situation after the payback period, and the return on capital invested.

Average rate of return

This method calculates the average annual net cash inflow as a percentage of the initial cash outflow. This may be represented by the formula:

$$\frac{\text{Average annual net cash inflow}}{\text{Initial cash outlay}}$$

This provides an entirely different kind of yardstick, which indicates the return earned on the capital employed. This method also has the advantage of simplicity, but continues to ignore the timing of cash flows.

Net present value

Money can be said to have a time value. One pound today is worth more than £1 in a year's time because it can be invested to earn interest. How much more it is worth will depend upon the rate of interest it can earn during the year. If it can be used to buy stocks or bonds paying ten per cent per annum, then it will be worth £1.10 in one year's time. Expressed another way, £1 received in one year's time is equivalent to 91p today (91p + 10% = £1.)

To arrive at a proper appraisal an allowance must be made for the timing of cash flows, and this is done by reducing the value of future incomings and outgoings to their present-day worth, using an appropriate rate of interest. This process is known as 'discounting' and the factors may be calculated using the formula:

$$\frac{1}{(1 + n_i)}$$

where 'i' is the rate of interest and 'n' the number of years. In practice, it is much easier to look up the figures in discounting tables.

To provide an additional assessment of the merits of each investment, the discounted inflows can be related to the original outlay to complete what is known as the 'profitability index'. The project with the highest profitability index is to be preferred.

	10 % Discount £	Machine A		Machine B		Machine C	
		Actual value £	Present value £	Actual value £	Present value £	Actual value £	Present value £
Initial cash outflow	I	50,000	50,000	50,000	50,000	70,000	70,000
Net cash inflows							
Year							
1	.909	5,000	4,545	15,000	13,635	10,000	9,090
2	.826	10,000	8,260	25,000	20,650	10,000	8,260
3	.751	15,000	11,265	15,000	11,265	20,000	15,020
4	.683	20,000	13,660	5,000	3,415	20,000	13,660
5	.621	20,000	12,420	5,000	3,105	30,000	18,630
6	.564	15,000	8,460	–	–	20,000	11,280
7	.513	–	–	–	–	10,000	5,130
Residual value		1,000	564	–	–	2,000	1,026
		86,000	59,174	65,000	52,070	122,000	82,092

Yield or internal rate of return

This is a refinement of the last method. It is used when managers wish to know the discount rate which exactly equates cash inflows with the outlay. This is sometimes to be preferred to assuming a rate.

The calculation is more time-consuming as it involves using a trial and error method on at least two rates until the two figures are equal. This rate can then be compared with, say, the rate of any borrowed money which may be required to finance the project or the company's average cost of capital.

Year	Cash flow	Discounted at 14%		Discounted at 16%	
		Factor	Present value	Factor	Present value
1	5,000	.877	4,385	.862	4,310
2	10,000	.769	7,690	.743	7,430
3	15,000	.675	10,125	.641	9,615
4	20,000	.592	11,840	.552	11,040
5	20,000	.519	10,380	.476	9,520
6	15,000	.456	6,840	.410	6,150
Residual value	1,000	.456	456	.410	410
	86,000		51,716		48,475

The correct rate of return lies somewhere between the two and may be determined by interpolation:

$$14 + \frac{51,716}{51,716 + 48,475} \times 2 = 15.03\%$$

Shortcomings of appraisal methods

Having completed an example of capital investment appraisal, one shortcoming is immediately obvious: all methods do not give the same answer. The final choice must be made in the light of all the circumstances. It is a matter for managerial judgement as to whether the security of a short payback outweighs the disadvantage of lower profitability.

The forecasting of cash flows can also pose serious problems. Because of the longer-term nature of most capital investment it is often extremely difficult to project timings and amounts for cash inflows and outflows, particularly during the later stages of the project. This can easily render any appraisal meaningless. Delays in installation of even comparatively simple machinery can quickly cause large variances from the plan, and escalating costs can rapidly eat up margins. In many cases, some proportion of the net cash inflows is represented by expected cost savings, and these are often much more difficult to realise in practice than they are on paper. The machine which was intended to dispense with the services of ten operatives and increase productivity by 30 per cent often looks much less economical after the first year of operation.

It is vital to take all cash items into account when completing the appraisal. It is easy to forget the cost of any additional working capital the project may require, particularly in the area of work-in-progress. Occasionally, new equipment can provide a reduction in the need for working capital and this should not be overlooked as a cash inflow or lower cash outflow.

MONITORING LIQUIDITY

Monthly current asset and liability figures (as well as monitoring business performance through ratio analysis, cash flow and management information) can be utilised to help monitor the corporate cash flow movements.

Corporate managers will frequently encounter situations where the company has executed a debenture charge to the bank. This type of security will give the bank differing priorities over the company assets. Forms of charge vary between banks but a debenture usually gives the bank the following security:

- a legal mortgage over all freehold and leasehold property together with buildings, fixtures and fixed plant and machinery;
- an equitable fixed first charge on after-acquired property including fixed plant and machinery;
- a fixed first charge on present book debts and future book debts;
- a first floating charge over all the other assets of the company, both present and future.

The debenture usually specifies within the charge form the right to appoint a receiver after demand for payment of monies secured or at the request of the company's directors.

The receiver's powers will generally include the right to:

- take possession of and sell off assets;
- carry on the business and borrow money on the security of the assets;
- appoint managers and agents to assist with running the business;
- carry out acts incidental to the performance of these duties.

Limitations of the charge

Any preferential creditors, e.g. VAT or PAYE, will erode available floating charge recoveries. However, a bank can rank in priority with other preferentials in respect of advances for wages and salaries. Under the UK Insolvency Act 1986 (Section 6, para. 11), money advanced and actually paid to employees during the four months prior to winding-up will be valid subject to a maximum of £800 in respect of each employee.

Furthermore under S.245 of the UK Insolvency Act 1986, floating charges granted within twelve months prior to the commencement of winding-up are invalid unless it can be proved that the company was solvent at the time the charge was created. However, bank debt will often have been turned over by receipts and payments through the account, and the advance will be deemed to represent new money. In these cases the floating charge will then be valid.

The bank setting a debenture formula

In setting a formula for cover of the bank debt by current assets, the bank will be considering both the balance sheet strength and the nature of the risk. For example, in the case of a long-established, successful business having substantial fixed assets, a finer margin of cover may be stipulated than for a relatively new, expanding business with few fixed assets.

Furthermore, regard will be given both to the annual accounts and also to the current levels of book debts to make sure that any formula set is workable. A formula could be two and a half times cover of the bank debt by stock plus debtors, with cover of one and a half times by book debts.

A further guide to workable formulae is to look at profit/cash budgets and derive from them a monthly projected balance sheet to test the anticipated coverage position.

There are many possible variations of the formula, but whatever the margin of cover decided upon, corporate managers should be aware that any breach of the set formula may be used by the banker as a 'trigger' to call for interim financial accounts or call for a fresh review of the company's affairs by an independent firm of accountants.

AGREED FORMULA; 2.5 × debtors + stock	COMPANY NAME; ABC	FINANCIAL YEAR END............. 31 December					
	From ann. accounts	From company books:					
	31.12.X5 £	Jan £	Feb £	Mar £	Apr £	May £	Jun £
Current assets							
Cash	2,500.0	1,800	2,600	1,500	2,800	3,200	1,800
Debtors	484,500.0	472,653	486,152	517,250	586,220	570,185	526,590
Stock	120,000.0	135,500	140,200	120,700	115,800	112,100	110,500
Total (A)	607,000.0	609,953	628,952	639,450	704,820	685,485	638,890
Current liabilities							
Bank	115,850.0	108,950	120,680	105,700	102,800	100,849	98,774
Creditors	192,180.0	210,525	200,520	225,600	210,723	202,576	197,821
Total (B)	308,030.0	319,475	321,200	331,300	313,523	303,425	296,595
Net of totals (A–B)	298,970.0	290,478	307,752	308,150	391,297	382,060	346,795
Cap. exp.-disposals	10,000.0						30,000
Sales record	2.4	215,280	325,650	350,320	325,000	328,520	255,650

Fig 3.11 Monitoring Form

Monitoring

To enable effective monitoring of the formula it is advisable to use some kind of debenture monitoring form. A suggested layout is shown in Figure 3.11. With such a form the listing of figures for debtors, stock, creditors, etc. from the latest available annual accounts forms a useful base for comparison with current figures on a month by month basis. The bank balances used should be as per the company's books. Sales per annum and sales per month need to be included. This information will enable the monitoring of current sales activity. Capital expenditures or disposals should be minuted as they will have an effect on liquidity movements. The current assets total should then be compared with the agreed lending cover formula to ensure compliance with the agreed covenants between the company and the bank.

CRITICAL ANALYSIS OF VARIATIONS

As well as monitoring the debenture cover formula of bank debt to current assets, the monitoring form is also useful in highlighting the net current asset movement position (net of totals: A–B), as Figure 3.11 shows.

In this case the formula was $2\frac{1}{2}$ times cover by debtors and stock which was easily maintained each month. The net current assets position (A–B) shows an improving trend from January to May but suddenly drops back in June. Why did this occur? Enquiries reveal that £30,000 was spent on a new machine.

Comparing the June end position with the opening figures shows an improvement of (£376,795–£298,970). Although this does not always represent a profit figure, it does show as a healthy sign. This positive movement can only be caused by profits earned, funds injected, sale of fixed assets or a combination of all three. Equally, if the movement was negative (as occurred from May to June), further enquiry would be justified.

The annual sales of £2.4 million average out to £200,000 per month. Monthly sales recorded on the form look good in comparison, and it will be interesting to see the full twelve months' picture. Sales also show a seasonality trend with peak sales in March.

Additional analysis

You will have seen how important it is to understand fully the figures presented on the liquidity monitoring form. For this reason it is suggested that the following additional analyses are made.

Debtors

This figure needs breaking down into normal trade, inter-company, and doubtful debts. Care should be taken not to include any debts which have been factored under a factoring agreement. Further, it is useful to get an indication of debtor spread and debtor control as shown below.

DEBTOR ANALYSIS

DEBTOR	TOTALS	AGE (days)				REMARKS
		Current	30	60	90	
£1000 and over						
Others						
PERCENTAGES	100%	%	%	%	%	

DEBTOR ANALYSIS BY MAJOR CUSTOMER ACCOUNT

NAME	Total balance	Current	30 days	60 days	90 days	REMARKS
Totals						

Stock

This figure is a difficult one for many businesses to provide. Frequently there will be many differing stock-lines and the only accurate way to determine levels is to carry out a physical stock-check. This difficulty can be overcome if the stock-file is computerised.

A further complication arises in businesses where there is on-going product manufacture or job contracts – then it will also be necessary to estimate work-in-progress.

Stock can be invoiced from a supplier subject to reservation of title (Romalpa terms). This reservation means that goods supplied remain the property of the supplier until he is paid. Again the directors should provide details. The table below illustrates stock analysis.

ANALYSIS OF MANUFACTURING STOCK

	Month ended . . .	
Stock	£	as a %
Raw materials		
Work in progress		
Finished goods		
Total stock*		
*Reservation of title £ . . .		

It is useful, when stock is physically checked and valued, to mark the stock figure on the debenture monitoring form accordingly.

Creditors

In addition to age analysis as shown opposite, which indicates if there is pressure for payment on the business, it is also very useful to split the creditors' total into normal trade and preferential. We are very interested in the preferential creditors for the reasons stated at the beginning when we considered the debenture charge and realisation issues.

We should establish if there are any set-off trading positions between creditors and debtors which might lead to counter-claims.

CREDITOR ANALYSIS

CREDITOR	TOTALS	AGE				REMARKS
		Current	30	60	90	
£1000 and over						
Others						
PERCENTAGES	100 %	%	%	%	%	

CREDITOR ANALYSIS BY MAJOR CUSTOMER ACCOUNT

CREDITOR	TOTALS	AGE				REMARKS
		Current	30	60	90	
Trade:						
Preferential creditors VAT PAYE/NIC etc.						
TOTALS						

LIQUIDITY OUT OF CONTROL

If all parties are slightly unsure of their ground, then a useful step is to agree to the appointment of an investigating accountant. His brief will vary but essentially it is to:

- comment on and analyse recent trading;
- draw up a current statement of affairs;
- comment on the future viability and cash flow of the business;
- comment on the bank exposure and security.

The appointee should be an accountant with proven expertise and if possible knowledge of the particular trade.

The investigation can be quick as it may only take from three to five days to get a 'feel' for the business and make a preliminary report. The company directors should cooperate, as it is also in their interest to know where they stand.

The following case study will illustrate the speed with which a liquidity position can deteriorate.

Case study: M Group Ltd

This group was involved in cash and carry wines and spirits with three warehouses and six retail shops. The business commenced in 1960 and had grown rapidly in recent years. The board of four directors included the proprietor and his wife, a sales director and a chartered accountant acting as finance director.

They had been unable to produce recent liquidity figures due to the company transferring its records to computer. There had been pressure of late on the bank account and although the company directors were concerned about this, they felt that it was only temporary and was mainly caused by the cost of a move of premises.

However, draft accounts were produced to the company year-end at 31 March, and when compared with previous years, the following was revealed:

	Draft Accounts 19X3	Audited accounts 19X4	19X5	31.3.X6
Sales	£9.3m	£19m	£30.4m	£36.1m
Gross profit	£586,000	£909,000	£1.3m	£1.2m
Gross profit %	6.2%	4.8%	4.2%	3.4%
Overheads	£485,000	£689,000	£1.1m	£1.7m
Profit (loss)	£101,000	£220,000	£147,000	(£484,000)

The group results indicate the rapid growth of the business in the last four years, with sales going from £9.3 million to £36.1 million, and with a fine (and deteriorating) gross margin, down from 6.2% to 3.4%.

The draft accounts also reveal both a drop in gross margin and at the same time increased overheads, to £1.7 million, resulting in a loss of £484,000.

With the move of premises and transfer to computer, no management accounts were prepared during the latter part of the year to 31.3.X6, and consequently the considerable loss came as a shock to the directors.

The directors agreed to the appointment of investigating accountants to try to pinpoint the current trading position and cash flow requirement. The accountants subsequently reported:

- a serious imbalance of trade between volume of sales, gross margins and overheads incurred;
- that the accounting records maintained were most inadequate for a business of this nature with fine gross margins and high volume of turnover.

The accountants also made the following report:

The group business has such a high turnover of stocks with very short periods of credit given and taken that the balance sheet can change dramatically in short periods of time. This is highlighted by the reduction of surplus on the bank's charge on a going concern basis between 31/3 and 20/5 from £4.8 million to £2.4 million.

In our view the liquidity position is not satisfactory . . . the company can never be sure as to what the position is . . .

Losses are highly likely to be continuing . . .

A few weeks later a receiver was appointed.

CASH RECEIPTS FROM BREAK-UP VALUES

What can be recovered as a percentage of book debts, stock or fixed assets varies enormously from trade to trade and area to area. Full recovery on each asset is rare.

Here is an interesting case study that shows what can happen.

Case study: Company X

Company X were UK distributors for domestic kitchen appliances. Sales were mainly to electrical wholesalers and kitchen specialists. The goods carried no manufacturer's guarantee but were distributed by Company X with their own twelve month warranty.

Company X traded profitably in its early years but later incurred substantial losses due to abortive ventures into new kitchen and bathroom products. At the same time high warranty charges were encountered with one major product line and business overheads also increased during 19X1 and 19X2:

Year ended December:	19W9	19X0	19X1	19X2
Sales	£2.57m	£3.56m	£4.23m	£2.3m
Gross profit%	19%	18%	18%	17%
Overheads	£493,000	£641,000	£965,000	£783,000
Overheads/sales %	19%	18%	23%	34%
Net profit/(loss)	–	–	(£202,000)	(£323,000)

Investigating accountants were called in in September 19X3 (after the bank received the disastrous 19X2 trading figures) and reported that the bank debt should be covered on a break-up basis:

ESTIMATED STATEMENT OF AFFAIRS AS AT 30.9.X3

	Book value	Break-up value
	£000	£000
Assets subject to fixed charge:		
Debtors	425	335
Less: Bank	(393)	(393)
Surplus/(shortfall) to debenture holder under fixed charge	32	(58)
Assets subject to floating charge:		
Stock	497	251
Plant/machinery/motor vehicles	33	15
	530	266

		Book value	Break-up value
		£000	£000
Preferential creditors			
PAYE/NI		36	
Rates		12	
VAT	130		
Employees (holiday pay)	3		
		(181)	(181)
Surplus available under floating charge		349	85
Surplus/(shortfall) to debenture holder b/f		32	(58)
		381	27
Unsecured creditors		(553)	(553)
Shortfall to unsecured creditors		(172)	(526)

You will see that most of the bank's cover was on book debts as a fixed charge.

When receivership took place later in December 19X3 the bank's cover on debtors was quickly dissipated with many counter-claims from customers on warranty work and also retentions in case of future warranty complaints.

Finally, by 19X6 the total recovery from book debts amounted to only £134,000 as against the initial book value of £425,000.

Stock also suffered, although previously discounted by 50% to £251,000. Eventual realisation was only £125,000 (50% of the discounted figure).

Conclusion

Here are some thoughts on the management of cash flow.

Cash flow does not flow of its own accord – it can only do so as a direct consequence of management decisions . . . taken either consciously and positively or unconsciously by default. This summarises those major management decision areas which cause cash to flow:

(1) Operating decisions – the range of decisions which contribute to profit before changing depreciation: cash flow from operations.
(2) Capital expenditure decisions – the acquisition or disposal of plant, equipment or such other assets of a long lasting nature which result in a depreciation charge against profits.
(3) Stock decisions – changes in the amounts tied up in stocks of raw materials, finished goods, work-in-progress, sub-assemblies, spares etc. Increases in stock create a negative cash flow; decreases a positive cash flow.

(4) Customer credit decisions – the length of time customers are permitted to take before paying up. An increase in customer credit delays cash inflow; a reduction accelerates it.

(5) Supplier credit policies – the length of time taken before payment for materials, services and other items. An increase in supplier credit effectively creates a positive cash flow in that it delays cash outflow; a reduction of credit accelerates cash outflow.

(6) Other accepted credit terms – e.g. rent, telephone, electricity and certain taxes (such as VAT settlement), where it is normal to pay at periodic intervals in arrears.

(7) Tax on Corporate profit payable at certain dates, predetermined by law, has a significant impact upon the pattern of cash outflows.

(8) Financial obligations – interest & dividend payments plus any contractual payments of Capital arising from past financing decisions.
    The impact of the decision areas will determine the net cash surplus or deficit any any point in time which leads to:

(9) Investment decisions – the utilisation of surplus cash by the purchase of investments or, conversely, the liberation of cash by sale of such investments.

(10) Financing decisions – the aquisition of new money either from shareholders or by borrowing (including instalment purchasing, hire purchase or leasing to finance capital expenditure).

In this chapter we looked at ways of squeezing out more cash and examined:

- what is operational cash flow and why it is important in cash management;
- we then linked this analysis into break-even and the margin of safety in terms of business revenues and cash flow fall-back positions;
- next we examined the business cycle and the importance of understanding this in order to see the consumption or generation rates of cash flow and thereby gain an understanding of the financial structuring necessary to underpin the business;
- an analysis was made of the risks inherent within the cash flow cycles and comparisons made of timing issues;
- contrasting cash flow profiles were featured in two examples of a large food retailing group and a heavy engineering manufacturing business;
- an introduction was made to capital investment methods of appraisal, reviewing four main methods of assessment;
- the important aspect of monitoring liquidity was our next topic and analysis was made of the key areas of debtors, stock and trade credit;
- finally we looked at a case study featuring liquidity out of control and asset break-up collection values and cash received on disposal.

4

CASH FLOW – FORECASTING

In any corporate, planning for future liquidity is essential. Cash flow fore-casting will require little introduction to most business people. It is easy for the bank or equity investor to say '**Please prepare a cash forecast for the next twelve months'**. However the compilation of the document can be a long and arduous process.

All businesses must of course preserve liquidity in order to meet cash commitments to creditors, employees and shareholders. A good forward order book will be useless if we don't have the cash needed to finance the production of our products. The ability therefore to be able to forecast cash movements and then **monitor progress** is a key requirement in business planning.

A good way to start is by completing a cash flow worksheet (Fig 4.1).

If your company sells mainly on credit, then the analysis of collections will be of crucial importance. However if you are selling mainly for cash, then more focus will be needed on disbursements. It's a question of fully analysing the cash profile of your business and committing it to the work-sheet.

The issue of longer term forecasts will be looked at later in this section.

From the worksheet you can then evolve a monthly cash flow forecast and predict when cash will enter and leave your bank account. **You will then know when it is best to purchase new equipment, take on more staff etc.**

We can now put this into practice by looking at two example case studies. Both will illustrate the importance of good cash flow planning in order to attract investors/financiers and to ensure an adequate payback period.

	JAN.	FEB.	MAR.	APR.	MAY.	JUN.	JUL.	AUG.	SEP.	OCT.	NOV.	DEC.
1. Cash in bank (start of month)												
2. Petty cash (start of month)												
3. Total cash (add 1 & 2)												
4. Expected cash sales												
5. Expected collections												
6. Other money expected												
7. Total receipts (add 4, 5 & 6)												
8. Total cash & receipts (add 3 & 7)												
9. All disbursements (for month)												
10. Cash balance at end of month (subject 9 from 8)*												

* This balance is your starting balance for the next month.

Fig 4.1 Cash Flow Worksheet

CASE STUDY:
HOTEL PROJECT – HONG KONG HOTEL CO. LTD

Background

This case focusses on the construction of a new hotel in Hong Kong for which cash forecasts will be essential.

The shareholders of the Hotel Co. are a group operating under the control of a well known businessman. The group has extensive experience in *hotel operation, and manages a five-star hotel 'XYZ Hotel' in TST, Kowloon. They also have a bank loan facility of over $100 million.*

Four years ago, Hotel Co. Ltd bought a piece of land in Mongkok to build a three-star hotel. The total area of the land was 80,000 square feet, with around 200 rooms planned when the hotel was completed. At the beginning, the land was used as the security to borrow a total of $78 million from a bank. On the cash forecast the company will use $68 million to cover the cost of land, construction, electronic engineering, interior renovation etc, while the remaining $10 million will be used as the interest payment and for miscellaneous expenses before the opening of the hotel. However, two years ago, the company requested an increase in the loans by $30 million to a total of $108 million, in view of increases in construction costs. In other words, 70% of the budgeted cost of the new hotel project was financed by way of loans from the bank.

The company was given an 18 months grace period to repay the loan after the building occupation permit was issued. The company should pay the premium after each three months (in 28 instalments) and the interest should be payable on a monthly basis. The three-star hotel was opened about one year ago and named as 'ABC Hotel'.

Application for the bank loans and method of repayment

The hotel has an average monthly income of about $4 million, enough to support the daily cash flow. However, the hotel may need some money for contingencies, so a $1 million overdraft was applied for at the bank. This uses the Prime Rate as their interest rate.

Because of the cost over-runs in the construction stage, the shareholders had already injected $8 million into the hotel. The hotel will use its surplus to repay the shareholders. Recently, the hotel borrowed $8 million from the bank to repay all the loans from shareholders. The terms of the $8 million loans are:

- payment schedule of 20 instalments (three months)
- interest rate: HIBOR (Hong Kong Inter Bank Offered Rate) + 1.5%.

DETAILS OF THE LENDINGS

			Repayment Schedule	Interest Rate
Secured loans	108	$108m	28 quarters	HIBOR+3/4%
Overdraft	1		$1m on demand	Prime Rate
Unsecured	8		$8m 20 quarters	HIBOR+1.5%
Total	117			$117m

Note Security: 1. Debenture incorporating a Legal Charge of 'ABC Hotel' and Floating Charge
(Banking Facilities - HK$ 108 million.)
2. Subordination and Assignment of Loan.

Evaluation needed of key factors that will affect cash flow:

- The likely level of occupancy of the hotel rooms;
- Market trends of hotel and tourist industry in Hong Kong;
- The cash flow forecast timings and its projected income/costs;
- Ability of the hotel to repay the additional loans out of expected cash flow;
- The experience of the business people and the relationship between the client and the bank.

Occupancy rate of the ABC Hotel

Hotel occupancy levels in Hong Kong are affected by seasonal factors such as the Chinese Export Commodities Fair in Guang Zhou, and by the direction of China's reform policy, etc. It is essential therefore to factor in these issues when estimating the occupancy rate of ABC Hotel.

According to the following figures, the average occupancy rate of ABC Hotel is about 80%. However we are told that the average occupancy rate since opening is about 72%. We can observe that after one year's operation of this new hotel, the business is running quite smoothly and we can expect that the hotel will have an improving occupancy rate.

HOTEL ROOM OCCUPANCY RATE BY MONTH

HOTEL OCCUPANCY (%)

	HKTA Member[1] Hotels		XYZ Hotel[2]	ABC Hotel 1992–1993 (Forecast)
	1989	1990	1991	
Jan	88	70	89.9	75.25 (1993)
Feb	75	77	52.4	67.93 (1993)
Mar	86	80	62.8	73.00 (1993)
Apr	88	81	81.3	83.30 (1992)
May	83	75	72.8	78.85 (1992)
Jun	76	77	83.9	83.85 (1992)
Jul	71	76	73.4	77.47 (1992)
Aug	72	77	89.4	81.03 (1992)
Sep	76	79	82.2	82.47 (1992)
Oct	81	86	90.5	88.54 (1992)
Nov	82	87	91.1	91.24 (1992)
Dec	75	78	76.4	77.07 (1992)
AVG.	79.4	78.6	78.8	80.00

1. Statistics of the member hotels of the Hong Kong Travelling Association.
2. XYZ Hotel is the sister hotel of ABC Hotel.

According to the statistics in 1989 and 1990, the occupancy rate of the medium tariff hotels is below 80%. It is acceptable therefore that ABC Company have predicted the occupancy rate at 80% in 1993.

The table overleaf shows that according to the actual income of ABC Hotel the proportion of room sales is higher than for other hotels. However, sales of food and beverages are lower. This is because ABC Hotel is not located in the central business and shopping area, and so, compared to hotels that are sited in the business district, food and beverage sales form a smaller proportion of total sales, leaving room sales playing a much more important part in ABC's income.

INCOME ANALYSIS ON ABC HOTEL

PERCENTAGE DISTRIBUTION OF HOTEL REVENUE

	HKTA Member Hotels		XYZ Hotel 1991	ABC Hotel (Projection)	ABC Hotel (Actual)
	1989	1990			
Total revenue:					
Room sales	58.50%	56.40%	58.63%	62.71%	63.07%
Food & beverage sales	31.60%	33.10%	31.32%	20.81%	22.20%
Minor operated dept. sales	3.90%	4.20%	2.22%	0.67%	0.67%
Telephone sales	3.50%	3.70%	5.70%	6.04%	6.26%
Rentals & other income	2.50%	2.60%	2.13%	9.77%	7.80%
	100.00%	100.00%	100.00%	100.00%	100.00%

The table also shows that the projected income of ABC Hotel is close to the actual income. The hotel, which has $29.56 million of real income from opening, is also averaging $2.69 million per month. It is predicted that total income will be $40.58 million per month, representing an average income of $.38 million – an increase of 26% per month on past real income.

It should be noted that the income of ABC Hotel also includes the rental received from a restaurant.

MARKET TRENDS: TOURISM AND VISITORS TO HONG KONG

Place of origin	February 92	February 91	increase (%)
South East Asia	71,404	47,009	+ 51.9
Taiwan	120,879	106,653	+ 13.3
Japan	107,845	73,097	+ 47.5

North America	53,729	40,735	+ 31.9
Western Europe	59,014	46,910	+ 25.8
Australia/New Zealand	16,932	15,330	+ 10.5
Other	46,572	35,688	+ 30.5
Total	476,375	365,422	+ 30.4

According to the above table, there was an average 30.4% increase in visitors to Hong Kong. The most rapid growth is in the visitors from South East Asia and Japan. However, the largest number of visiting foreigners are from Taiwan and Japan.

ABC Hotel is a 3-star hotel. The target customers are visitors from Japan, Taiwan and South East Asia, so a 26% increase in monthly income projected is probably acceptable.

According to the above table the marketing segment is as follows:

Place	% of the whole market
Taiwan	25.4%
Japan	22.6%
South East Asia	15.0%
Western Europe	12.4%
North America	11.3%
Australia/New Zealand	3.5%
Other	9.8%
	100%

Analysis of cash flow

The projected cash flow statement of ABC Hotel is as follows:

ABC HOTEL – CASH FLOW 4/92 TO 3/93

HKD'000

	Apr 92	May 92	Jun 92	Jul 92	Aug 92	Sep 92	Oct 92	Nov 92	Dec 92	Jan 93	Feb 93	Mar 93	Total
Total revenue	3,335	3,280	3,414	3,248	3,435	3,321	4,219	4,191	3,244	3,128	2,609	3,156	40,580
Total expense	(3,294)	(3,279)	(3,325)	(3,358)	(3,332)	(3,305)	(3,351)	(3,352)	(3,340)	(3,277)	(3,226)	(3,030)	(39,469)
Operation profit	41	1	89	(110)	103	16	839	839	(96)	(149)	(617)	126	1,111
Less: capital expenditure	(119)	(119)	(119)	(119)	(119)	(119)	(119)	(119)	(119)	(119)	(119)	(118)	(1,427)
Add : depreciation	578	578	579	578	578	579	578	578	579	578	578	579	6,940
Add : amortization of pre-opening exp.	114	114	113	114	114	113	114	114	113	114	114	113	1,364
Surplus/(deficit)	614	574	662	463	676	589	1,441	1,412	447	424	(44)	700	7,988
Balance C/f	0	614	1,188	1,850	2,313	2,989	3,578	5,019	6,431	6,908	7,332	7,288	—
Balance B/f	614	1,188	1,850	2,313	2,989	3,578	5,019	6,431	6,908	7,332	7,288	7,988	7,988
Less: interest exp.	(643)	(664)	(643)	(652)	(652)	(632)	(640)	(620)	(640)	(628)	(569)	(628)	(7,611)
Surplus/(deficit)	(29)	(90)	19	(189)	24	(43)	801	792	(163)	(204)	(613)	72	377
Balance C/f	0	(29)	(119)	(100)	(289)	(265)	(308)	493	1,235	1,122	918	305	—
Balance B/f	(29)	(119)	(100)	(289)	(265)	(308)	493	1,285	1,122	918	305	377	377
Less: loan repayment	0	0	0	(2,025)	0	0	(2,025)	0	0	(2,025)	0	0	(6,075)
Surplus/(deficit)	(29)	(90)	19	(2,214)	24	(43)	(1,224)	792	(163)	(2,229)	(613)	72	(5,698)
Balance C/f	0	(29)	(119)	(100)	(2,314)	(2,290)	(2,333)	(3,557)	(2,765)	(2,928)	(5,157)	(5,770)	—
Balance B/f	(29)	(119)	(100)	(2,314)	(2,290)	(2,333)	(3,557)	(2,765)	(2,928)	(5,157)	(5,770)	(5,698)	(5,698)

Conclusion

According to the cash flow statement of ABC Hotel, the cash flow is accept-able, and so the bank decided to grant a $5,000,000 overdraft. The bank was satisfied, based on the market research and the experience of the business people, that the cash flow assumptions were reasonable and therefore the financing went ahead. The verification of the 'top' line in any forecast is therefore a key issue!

In the next case we will look in more detail at the development period cash flows as well as the operational cash flows.

CASE STUDY:
MALAYSIAN CULTURE CENTRE (MCC) PROJECT

Part I (April 1989)

You have been called in as a cash flow specialist to look at this project and you have just attended a board meeting of the KL (Kuala Lumpur) Archaeo-logical Trust.

Planning is at an advanced stage to reconstruct an historic village on a site just within the city boundaries. The scheme will be located in an area where numerous artefacts have been found and it is thought that this will add real-ism to the project.

The design is imaginative with audio-visual effects reconstructing village life as it could have been centuries ago. Construction and fitting out costings are available and included in the project document. There will also be a shop retailing associated souvenir items.

The total project cost is RM2.65 million and the banks will be requested to fund, in syndicate, two loans of RM700,000 to assist in the financing of the scheme.

Let us then examine the project in terms of the funding requirements and the cash flow needed to service and ultimately pay back the bank loans if these can be obtained to finance the project.

PROJECT DOCUMENTS MCC – APRIL 1989

Finance/Cash Flow　　　**Units 000s**

Development Period – 2 Years to 31st March 1991

(i) The finance/cash flow report last produced on the 24th August 1988 envisaged overall cash flow during the development period as follows:

Finance Available

Trust	250
Malaysian Promotion of Tourism Board	250
Donations (3 years at 250 per year)	750
Banks	1,400
	2,650

From this we can see that the Trust Board are injecting RM250 and the Tourist Board are supporting with a grant of RM250. However the project needs donations of RM750 which will need verification and also debt of RM1,400.The project gearing (debt to equity) is therefore adverse and it will be difficult to obtain funding.

The documents go on to show how these funds will be utilised:

To be Utilised

Structure:	
Fixed Price Contract – Booths	1,050
Fitting out costs:	
Per Flood & Wilson Report	
RM 926,000 at '1988' prices –	
adjusted for inflation at 10%	1,175
Professional Costs	250
Costs of Development Team	75
Promotional Expenditure	60
	2,610

Notes on the development period:

(a) There is a very small surplus (2,650–2,610) of 40,000 between the funding and the projected spending;

(b) It should be noted that there is a maximum permissible 10% over-run on Building Contract to be funded by Archaeological Trust.

(ii) The contractor, Booths, has proposed as a condition that the initial 0.5 million provided by Trust/MPTB is to be applied directly to their structural contract with them additionally having first call on the donations to satisfy the balance of that contract.

The effect was that, of the RM2.65 million available, including donations of 0.75 million, 1.05 million is directed to Booths leaving 1.6 million to cover the cost of fitting out, the professional costs and the promotional expenditure.

(iii) The unknown factor required to 'balance the books' is the figure for donations. The passage of time from August 1988 to April 1989 has, in one sense, worked against the project in that there are now only two years before the planned opening date. On the other hand there are firmer indications that an annual figure of RM250,000 is achievable. The August 1988 Board's Report included the comment that 'in the event of donations not being received, the only course open to the MCC would be to economise on the fitting out costs'. This comment is as valid now as it was then.

(iv) On the basis that only two years' donations (0.25m × 2 = 0.5m) are now possible, the overall funds available in the development period shrink from 2.65 million to 2.4 million.

(v) As regards the development/capital cost of the project, there are two principal points:
(a) the possibility of a re-negotiation of structure costs with Booths;
(b) the apparent inadequacy of the capital cost provision for the general display in the Centre.

(vi) The scope for re-negotiation with Booths is limited, but it is unquestionably accepted that, the better the content of the MCC, the better the chance of attaining the RM500,000 per annum visitor level originally forecast. This is a straightforward 'Value for Money' argument.

(vii) Revised budgets are now available to accommodate the figure of RM2.4 million and a detailed comparison is necessary.

	Original	Revised
(a) Booths Structural Costs	1,050	960
(Note: 10% permissible over-run	——	——
to be separately financed and		
therefore ignored in both cases)		
(b) Fitting out costs:		
Building Work		
and finishes	250	253
Air conditioning & Space Heating	215	226
Sprinkler System	19	–
Electrical Installation	161	124
Lift	46	–
Closed Circuit T/V	16	–
Burglar Alarm	5	7
Building Contractors	84	90
Rail Carriages	100	100
Graphics and Audio Visual	30	227
	926	1,009
Add: 'Inflation'	249	112
	1,175	1,121
(c) Professional Fees:		
Booths	120	120
Others	130	178
	250	298
(d) Development Team Costs	75	75
(c) Promotional Expenditure	60	60
TOTALS	2,610	2,514

(a) The shortfall of RM114,000 is to be met by the Trust leasing tangible equipment in the Carriages/Graphics and Audio Visual area to the MCC.

(b) There is currently the possibility that the final cost of the air conditioning can be contained at RM150,000 rather than at RM226,000. In this event the additional monies are to be allocated to the Carriages/Graphics and Audio Visual Effects giving a total 'Display' cost of:

Carriages		100
Graphics and Audio Visual		227
		——
		327
Add: Inflation		36
		——
		363
Add: Re-allocation	76	
Inflation	8	
	——	
		84
		——
		447
		——

(viii) The time scale for progress payments is infinitely arguable. For the purposes of the current exercise it is taken as follows:
(a) Structural Work – March 1989 to March 1990.
(b) Fitting out – April 1990 to March 1991.

	Structural Cost	Fitting Out Costs	Prof. Fees	Development Team	Promotional Expenses
Totals (incl. 10% over-run)	1,060	1,120	298	72	60
1989					
March	100				
April	100			3	
May	150			3	
June	150			3	
July	175			3	

August	100			3	
September	75			3	
October	50			3	
November	50			3	
December	50			3	
1990					
January	60			3	
February			120	3	
March				3	
April		80	12	3	
May		80	12	3	
June		80	12	3	
July		80	12	3	
August		100	16	3	
September		100	16	3	
October		100	16	3	
November		100	17	3	
December		100	16	3	
1991					
January		100	16	3	10
February		100	16	3	25
March		100	17	3	25
	1,060	1,120	298	72	60

The effect of these timings can be more easily studied by using the more normal cash flow format as shown Tables A, B and C.

Table A for example illustrates the Trust loan of RM250 coming in and capital expenditure of RM100 resulting in a net credit carried forward of RM150.

Table B shows the continuation of the picture with various movements taking place as per the project plans. The end position shows in March 1990 an end of month position of loans/overdrafts at:

Trust	350
Booths	210
Banks	152

Table C takes us on through to March 1991, again in line with timings of the project, and we can see the banks' credit lines have been fully drawn to RM1,397.3.

TABLE A: CASH FLOW DURING DEVELOPMENT PERIOD – MARCH 1989 TO MARCH 1991

1988/89	1988 April	May	June	July	August	September	October	November	December	1989 January	February	March
INCOME												
Credit Balance Forward												
MPTB Grant												
Trust Loan												250.0
Interest Earned												
Donations												250.0
EXPENDITURE												
Capital Expenditure												100.0
Development Team Costs												100.0
CREDIT BALANCE FORWARD												150.0
LOANS/OVERDRAFTS (Month end balances)												
Trust												
Booths												(250.0)
Banks												
ROLLED UP INTEREST												
Booths												
Banks												(250.0)

TABLE B: CASH FLOW DURING DEVELOPMENT PERIOD

1989/90	1989									1990		
	April	May	June	July	August	September	October	November	December	January	February	March
INCOME												
Credit Balance Forward	150.0	50.0										
MPTB Grant		250.0	150.0									
Transfers from Loans	3.0	3.0	3.0	3.0	3.0	3.0	3.0	3.0	3.0	3.0	3.0	3.0
			(4.0)	175.0	100.0	75.0	50.0	50.0	40.0 (240.0)	60.0	120.0	
Interest Earned			4.0									
Donations									250.0			
	153.0	303.0	153.0	178.0	103.0	78.0	53.0	53.0	53.0	63.0	123.0	3.0
EXPENDITURE												
Capital Expenditure	100.0	150.0	150.0	175.0	100.0	75.0	50.0	50.0	50.0	60.0	120.0	
Development Team Costs	3.0	3.0	3.0	3.0	3.0	3.0	3.0	3.0	3.0	3.0	3.0	3.0
	103.0	153.0	153.0	178.0	103.0	78.0	53.0	53.0	53.0	63.0	123.0	3.0
CREDIT BALANCE FORWARD	50.0	150.0	—	—	—	—	—	—	—	—	—	—
LOANS/OVERDRAFTS (Month end balances)												
Trust	(250.0)	(250.0)	(250.0)	(250.0)	(250.0)	(250.0)	(250.0)	(250.0)	(290.0)	(350.0)	(350.0)	(350.0)
Booths				(175.0)	(275.0)	(350.0)	(400.0)	(450.0)	(210.0)	(210.0)	(210.0)	(210.0)
Banks	(3.0)	(6.0)	(5.0)	(8.0)	(11.0)	(14.0)	(17.0)	(20.0)	(23.0)	(26.0)	(149.0)	(152.0)
ROLLED UP INTEREST												
Booths						(5.2)	(5.2)	(5.2)	(19.2)	(19.2)	(19.2)	(26.6)
Banks			(.1)	(.1)	(.1)	(.4)	(.4)	(.4)	(1.1)	(1.1)	(1.1)	(3.5)

TABLE C: CASH FLOW DURING DEVELOPMENT PERIOD

1990/91	1990									1991		
	April	May	June	July	August	September	October	November	December	January	February	March
INCOME												
Transfers from Loans	95.0	95.0	95.0	95.0	119.0	119.0	69.0	70.0	(210.0) (41.3) 70.3 250.0	129.0	144.0	145.0
Donations												
	95.0	95.0	95.0	95.0	119.0	119.0	69.0	70.0	69.0	129.0	144.0	145.0
EXPENDITURE												
Capital Expenditure	92.0	92.0	92.0	92.0	116.0	116.0	116.0	117.0	116.0	116.0	116.0	117.0
Development Team Costs	3.0	3.0	3.0	3.0	3.0	3.0	3.0	3.0	3.0	3.0	3.0	3.0
Leasing Finance							(50.0)	(50.0)	(50.0)			
Promotional Expenditure										10.0	25.0	25.0
	95.0	95.0	95.0	95.0	119.0	119.0	69.0	70.0	69.0	129.0	144.0	145.0
LOANS/OVERDRAFTS (Month end balances)												
Trust	(350.0)	(350.0)	(350.0)	(350.0)	(350.0)	(350.0)	(350.0)	(350.0)	(350.0)	(350.0)	(350.0)	(350.0)
Booths	(210.0)	(210.0)	(210.0)	(210.0)	(210.0)	(210.0)	(210.0)	(210.0)	–	–	–	–
Banks	(247.0)	(342.0)	(437.0)	(523.0)	(651.0)	(770.0)	(839.0)	(909.0)	(979.3)	(1108.3)	(1252.3)	(1397.3)
ROLLED UP INTEREST												
Booths	(26.6)	(26.6)	(34.0)	(34.0)	(34.0)	(41.3)	(41.3)	(41.3)	–	–	–	–
Banks	(3.5)	(3.5)	(12.1)	(12.1)	(12.1)	(31.0)	(31.0)	(31.0)	(58.4)	(58.4)	(58.4)	(96.8)
												1844.1

The effects of these development periods translate to a Balance Sheet position at 31st March 1991 as follows. Readers should note the fully drawn positions of the grant, donations and the banks:

BALANCE SHEET AT 31ST MARCH 1991

Development Expenditure

Structural		1,060.0
Fitting out	1,120.0	
Deduct: Assets leased	(150.0)	
	———	970.0
Professional Costs		298.0
Development Costs		72.0
Promotional Expenditure		60.0
		———
		2,460.0
Interest incurred during period	138.1	
Interest earned	(4.0)	
	———	134.1
		———
		2,594.1
Donations and Grants		
MPTB		250.0
Other		500.0
	———	750.0
		———
		1,844.1
		═══

Repayable Loans

Trust (No Interest)		350.0
Banks	1,397.3	
Add: Rolled up Interest	96.8	
	———	1,494.1
		———
		1,844.1
		═══

A major difficulty with financing projects such as this is of course the critical timings of events of a technical nature. This is even more true with bigger projects such as Eurotunnel – just completed with cost and time over-runs of 100%!

All these matters have huge impact on cash flow, particularly where there is significant debt as interest rolls up in an escalating manner before there is any sign of income coming on stream.

Let us take the project on and start examining the operational period.

Turning next to Tables D, E, F and G shown below, these feature the operating cash flows when the centre is open and detail the period from April 1991 to March 1995.

Table D shows month by month the percentage of total income. Readers will see that the summer months attract the highest level of admissions and the entry fees plus surplus sales income on the retail shop give a total cash inflow of RM910,000. From this there are total cash outflows of RM 628,300 giving cash surpluses to reduce the bank loans.

Tables E, F and G show continuing improvements in income and further reductions in the bank borrowing.

TABLE D: OPERATING CASH FLOW – 1991/1992

1991/92	1991 April	May	June	July	August	September	October	November	December	1992 January	February	March	Units 000s March	Totals
% of Total Income	%11.19	9.16	13.37	15.41	17.05	12.96	6.54	1.91	1.36	1.50	4.50	5.05		
Admissions (excluding VAT)	81.7	66.9	97.6	112.5	124.5	94.6	47.7	13.9	9.9	11.0	32.8	36.9		730.0
Surplus on Retail Shop	20.1	16.5	24.1	27.7	30.7	23.3	11.8	3.4	2.4	2.7	8.2	9.1		180.0
	101.8	83.4	121.7	140.2	155.2	117.9	59.5	17.3	12.3	13.7	41.0	46.0		910.0
Leasing Charges	(3.8)			(3.7)			(3.8)			(3.7)				(15.0)
Shop Rental	(8.7)			(8.8)			(8.7)			(8.8)				(35.0)
Payroll – Centre	(9.2)	(9.1)	(9.2)	(9.2)	(9.2)	(9.1)	(9.2)	(9.2)	(9.1)	(9.2)	(9.2)	(9.1)		(110.0)
Shop	(4.3)	(4.3)	(4.3)	(4.3)	(4.3)	(4.3)	(4.3)	(4.3)	(4.3)	(4.3)	(4.3)	(4.4)		(51.7)
Publicity	(10.4)	(10.4)	(10.3)	(10.3)	(10.3)	(10.3)	(10.3)	(10.3)	(10.3)	(10.3)	(10.3)	(10.3)		(123.8)
General Overheads	(24.4)	(24.4)	(24.4)	(24.4)	(24.4)	(24.4)	(24.4)	(24.4)	(24.4)	(24.4)	(24.4)	(24.4)		(292.8)
	(60.8)	(48.3)	(48.1)	(60.7)	(48.2)	(48.1)	(60.7)	(48.2)	(48.1)	(60.7)	(48.2)	(48.2)		(628.3)
Positive/(Negative) Cash Flow	41.0	35.1	73.6	79.5	107.0	69.8	(1.2)	(30.9)	(35.8)	(47.0)	(7.2)	(2.2)		281.7
Donations									250.0					250.0
Interest Charges			(54.4)			(49.3)			(45.6)			(41.6)		(190.9)
Overdraft/Loans brought forward	(1594.1)	(1553.1)	(1518.0)	(1498.8)	(1419.3)	(1312.3)	(1291.8)	(1293.0)	(1323.9)	(1155.3)	(1202.3)	(1209.5)		
OVERDRAFT/LOANS CARRIED FORWARD	(1553.1)	(1518.0)	(1498.8)	(1419.3)	(1312.3)	(1291.8)	(1293.0)	(1323.9)	(1155.3)	(1202.3)	(1209.5)	(1253.3)		340.8

NOTE: Interest Free 'Support Loan' 250,000 throughout the year.

TABLE E: OPERATING CASH FLOW – 1992/1993

1992/93	1992 April	May	June	July	August	September	October	November	December	1993 January	February	March	Units 000s Totals
% of Total Income	%11.19	9.16	13.37	15.41	17.05	12.96	6.54	1.91	1.36	1.50	4.50	5.05	
Admissions (excluding VAT)	89.9	73.5	107.4	123.7	136.9	104.2	52.5	15.3	10.9	12.0	36.1	40.6	803.0
Surplus on Retail Shop	22.1	18.1	26.5	30.5	33.8	25.7	12.9	3.8	2.7	3.0	8.9	10.0	198.0
	112.0	91.6	133.9	154.2	170.7	129.9	65.4	19.1	13.6	15.0	45.0	50.6	1001.0
Leasing Charges	(3.8)			(3.7)			(3.8)			(3.7)			(15.0)
Shop Rental	(8.7)			(8.8)			(8.7)			(8.8)			(35.0)
Payroll – Centre	(10.1)	(10.1)	(10.1)	(10.0)	(10.1)	(10.1)	(10.1)	(10.0)	(10.1)	(10.1)	(10.1)	(10.1)	(121.0)
Shop	(4.7)	(4.8)	(4.7)	(4.8)	(4.7)	(4.8)	(4.7)	(4.8)	(4.7)	(4.8)	(4.7)	(4.7)	(56.9)
Publicity & Promotion	(7.5)	(7.4)	(7.5)	(7.4)	(7.5)	(7.4)	(7.5)	(7.4)	(7.5)	(7.4)	(7.4)	(7.4)	(89.3)
General Overheads	(26.8)	(26.8)	(26.8)	(26.8)	(26.8)	(26.8)	(26.8)	(26.9)	(26.9)	(26.9)	(26.9)	(26.9)	(322.1)
	(61.6)	(49.1)	(49.1)	(61.5)	(49.1)	(49.1)	(61.6)	(49.1)	(49.2)	(61.7)	(49.1)	(49.1)	(639.3)
Positive/(Negative) Cash Flow	50.4	42.5	84.8	92.7	121.6	80.8	3.8	(30.0)	(35.6)	(46.7)	(4.1)	1.5	361.7
Interest Charges Overdraft			(40.6)			(33.9)			(28.6)			(32.7)	(135.8)
brought forward	(1209.5)	(1159.1)	(1116.6)	(1072.4)	(979.7)	(858.1)	(811.2)	(807.4)	(837.4)	(901.6)	(948.3)	(952.4)	
OVERDRAFT CARRIED FORWARD	(1559.1)	(1116.6)	(1072.4)	(979.7)	(858.1)	(811.2)	(807.4)	(837.4)	(901.6)	(948.3)	(952.4)	(938.6)	225.9

NOTE: Interest Free
'Support Loan' 250,000 throughout the year.

TABLE F: OPERATING CASH FLOW – 1993/1994

1993/94	1993 April	May	June	July	August	September	October	November	December	1994 January	February	March	Units 000s Totals
% of **Total Income**	%11.19	9.16	13.37	15.41	17.05	12.96	6.54	1.91	1.36	1.50	4.50	5.05	
Admissions (excluding VAT)	98.0	80.2	117.2	135.0	149.5	113.5	57.3	16.7	11.9	13.1	39.4	44.2	876.0
Surplus on Retail Shop	24.4	20.0	29.1	33.6	37.1	28.3	14.2	4.2	2.9	3.4	9.8	11.0	218.0
	122.4	100.2	146.3	168.6	186.6	141.8	71.5	20.9	14.8	16.5	49.2	55.2	1094.0
Leasing Charges	(3.8)			(3.7)			(3.8)			(3.7)			(15.0)
Shop Rental	(8.7)			(8.8)			(8.7)			(8.8)			(35.0)
Payroll – Centre	(11.0)	(11.1)	(11.1)	(11.1)	(11.1)	(11.1)	(11.1)	(11.1)	(11.1)	(11.1)	(11.1)	(11.1)	(133.1)
Shop	(5.3)	(5.3)	(5.2)	(5.2)	(5.2)	(5.2)	(5.2)	(5.2)	(5.2)	(5.2)	(5.2)	(5.2)	(62.6)
Publicity & Promotion	(8.1)	(8.1)	(8.2)	(8.2)	(8.2)	(8.2)	(8.2)	(8.2)	(8.2)	(8.2)	(8.2)	(8.2)	(98.2)
General Overheads	(29.5)	(29.5)	(29.6)	(29.5)	(29.5)	(29.6)	(29.5)	(29.5)	(29.6)	(29.5)	(29.5)	(29.5)	(354.3)
	(66.4)	(54.0)	(54.1)	(66.5)	(54.0)	(54.1)	(66.5)	(54.0)	(54.1)	(66.5)	(54.0)	(54.0)	(698.2)
Positive/(Negative) Cash Flow	56.0	46.2	92.2	102.1	132.6	87.7	5.0	(33.1)	(39.3)	(50.0)	(4.8)	1.2	395.8
Interest Charges		(32.6)				(24.8)			(18.5)			(22.5)	(98.4)
Overdraft brought forward	(983.6)	(927.6)	(881.4)	(821.8)	(719.7)	(587.1)	(524.2)	(519.2)	(552.3)	(610.1)	(660.1)	(664.9)	
OVERDRAFT CARRIED FORWARD	(927.6)	(881.4)	(821.8)	(719.7)	(587.1)	(524.2)	(519.2)	(552.3)	(610.1)	(660.1)	(664.9)	(686.2)	297.4

NOTE: Interest Free 'Support Loan' 250,000 throughout the year.

TABLE G: OPERATING CASH FLOW – 1994/1995

1994/95	1994 April	May	June	July	August	September	October	November	December	1995 January	February	March	Units 000s Totals
% of Total Income %	11.19	9.16	13.37	15.41	17.05	12.96	6.54	1.91	1.36	1.50	4.50	5.05	
Admissions (excluding VAT)	108.2	88.6	129.3	149.0	164.9	125.3	63.2	18.5	13.2	14.5	43.5	48.8	967.0
Surplus on Retail Shop	27.0	22.1	32.2	37.1	41.1	31.2	15.8	4.6	3.3	3.6	10.8	12.2	241.0
	135.2	110.7	161.5	186.1	206.0	156.5	79.0	23.1	16.5	18.1	54.3	61.0	1208.0
Leasing Charges	(3.8)			(3.7)			(3.8)			(3.7)			(15.0)
Shop Rental	(8.7)			(8.8)			(8.7)			(8.8)			(35.0)
Payroll - Centre	(12.2)	(12.2)	(12.2)	(12.2)	(12.2)	(12.2)	(12.2)	(12.2)	(12.2)	(12.2)	(12.2)	(12.2)	(146.4)
Shop	(5.7)	(5.8)	(5.7)	(5.8)	(5.7)	(5.7)	(5.7)	(5.8)	(5.7)	(5.8)	(5.7)	(5.7)	(68.9)
Publicity & Promotion	(9.0)	(9.0)	(9.0)	(9.0)	(9.0)	(9.0)	(9.0)	(9.0)	(9.0)	(9.0)	(9.0)	(9.0)	(108.0)
General Overheads	(32.5)	(32.5)	(32.5)	(32.4)	(32.5)	(32.5)	(32.5)	(32.4)	(32.5)	(32.5)	(32.5)	(32.4)	(389.7)
	(71.9)	(59.5)	(59.4)	(71.9)	(59.4)	(59.5)	(71.9)	(59.4)	(59.4)	(72.0)	(59.4)	(59.3)	(763.0)
Positive/(Negative) Cash Flow	63.3	51.2	102.1	114.2	146.6	97.0	7.1	(36.3)	(42.9)	(53.9)	(5.1)	1.7	445.0
Interest Charges			(21.9)			(12.8)			(5.3)			(9.1)	(49.1)
Overdraft brought forward	(686.2)	(622.9)	(571.7)	(491.5)	(377.3)	(230.7)	(146.5)	(139.4)	(175.7)	(223.9)	(277.8)	(282.9)	
OVERDRAFT CARRIED FORWARD	(622.9)	(571.7)	(491.5)	(377.3)	(230.7)	(146.5)	(139.4)	(175.7)	(223.9)	(277.8)	(282.9)	(290.3)	395.9

NOTE: Interest Free 'Support Loan' of 250,000 to be repaid early in 1995/96.

Part two – operational period

At the outset of the operational period the borrowings will be as follows:

	Capital	Rolled Up Interest
Trust	350	NIL
Banks	1,397.3	96.8

With regard to donations it is anticipated that the impetus can be carried forward beyond the opening date and that a further RM250,000 will be received in 1991/92.

Exclusive of interest costs the level of operational expenditure stands as shown in appendices 'C' and 'D' below:-

	1991/92
Payroll – Centre	110.0
Shop	51.7
General Overheads	292.8
Publicity	123.8
	578.3

The adjusted shop rental will be at the rate of RM35,000 per annum and allowing for leasing charges on generous terms a further RM15,000 must be added for this item, giving a total overhead of approximately RM630,000.

Finance charges in the first year of operation will amount to RM200,000.

Exclusive of donations, and to provide any reasonable year one reduction in the overall borrowings, the centre *must generate income in excess of RM900,000.*

Admissions/income

The basic assumptions in the 1988 Report were:

• annual admissions 500,000 people of whom 70% will be adult and 30% children;

- Prices taken at RM2.00 per adult and 1.30 per child in 1991/92 (*both figures exclusive of VAT*).

The project consultant's report makes the assumption that the figures of RM2.00 and 1.30 are *inclusive of VAT*. It further suggests that a conservative estimate of the admission level would be 300,000 per annum, quoting overall net revenue of 73% of adult prices. Bearing in mind the current estimate of overheads at RM630,000, plus finance costs of 200,000 the MCC project just cannot work on these figures viz:

300,000 people x RM2 x 73% =	438,000
Add: Estimated Shop Profits	135,000
	573,000
Annual Deficit	257,000
	830,000

Short of completely re-planning and considerably reducing the overhead level the basic assumption must be that the centre will attract 500,000 people. In order to provide some safety factor it is assumed in the following cash flow exercise that the admission prices are inclusive of VAT and that additional discounts will reduce the overall admission income to 73% of the adult prices (i.e. to RM730,000).

Current statistics for retail shop profits are more optimistic and a figure of 65c per capita has been taken in 1989 terms, adjusted as shown in Appendix 'B'.

Fully operational, and having serviced the loans at a constant 14% the centre should generate, on the above bases, positive cash flow as shown below, with the rising trend reflecting both the effects of inflation and the reducing borrowings over the period.

	Cash Flow	Donations	Total
1991/92	90.8	250.0	340.8
1992/93	225.9	–	225.9
1993/94	297.4	–	297.4
1994/95	395.9	–	395.9

The quarterly levels of bank borrowings plus the RM100,000 'back up' loan during the first four operational years will be as shown:

1991	March	(1,594.1)
	June	(1,498.8)
	September	(1,291.8)
	December	(1,155.3)
1992	March	(1,253.3)
	June	(1,072.4)
	September	(811.2)
	December	(901.6)
1993	March	(983.6)
	June	(821.8)
	September	(524.2)
	December	(610.1)
1994	March	(686.2)
	June	(491.5)
	September	(146.5)
	December	(223.9)
1995	March	(290.3)

Appendix 'A': income – admissions

	c. per person	
	Adults	Children
Admission prices in 1987	150	100
– Inflation to opening date in April	1991 (10% p.a.)	
1988	15	10
	165	110
1989	16	11
	181	121
1990	18	12

Admission Prices Ruling at Opening	200 (say)	130 (say)
– Inflation in first four operating years (10% p.a.)		
1991	20	13
	⎯⎯	⎯⎯
	220	143
1992	22	14
	⎯⎯	⎯⎯
	242	157
1993	24	16
	⎯⎯	⎯⎯
	266	173
1994	27	17
	⎯⎯	⎯⎯
	293	190

1991/92 500,000 x RM2.00 × 73% = 730
1992/93 500,000 x RM2.20 × 73% = 803
1993/94 500,000 x RM2.40 × 73% = 876
1994/95 500,000 x RM2.65 × 73% = 967

Appendix 'B': income – retail shop profits

Notes

- taken on the basis of 65c per capita in 1989 terms and applying an inflation factor of 10% during the construction and fitting out period the 65c will become 80c at the opening date in April 1991;
- the inflation factor in the first four operating years, again applied at 10% p.a. will give figures of:

Operating years to 31st March	*per Capita income*	*× 500,000 (Units RM000s)*
1992	80c	400
1993	88c	440
1994	97c	485
1995	107c	535

Gross Profit taken at an average 45% in the years ending 31st March

	(Units RM000s)
1992	180
1993	198
1994	218
1995	241

Appendix 'C' – expenditure

	CENTRE *Salary*	SHOP-DIRECT *Salary*
CATEGORY		
Administrative and Office:		
1 General Manager	11,000	
1 Book-keeper/Wages Clerk	4,500	
1 Secretary	3,500	
Curatorial Services:		
1 Curator	8,000	
1 Assistant	4,500	
Retail Shop:		
1 Shop Manager		7,000
4 Sales Assistants @ RM3,000		12,000
4 Part-time Assistants @ RM2,000		8,000
1 Storeman		4,000
Admission and Security:		
3 Admission Attendants @ RM2,500	7,500	
3 Security Attendants @ RM5,000	15,000	
Maintenance and Cleaning:		
1 Audio/Visual Technician	6,000	
1 Vehicle Maintenance Engineer	6,000	
TOTALS (1987 LEVELS)	66,000	31,000
Add 13.75% for Social Security etc.	9,075	4,262
	RM75,075	RM35,262

Appendix 'C' (continued): payroll/overheads

Units RM000s PAYROLL		TOTAL	
	Centre	Shop	Overheads
At 1987/88 levels	75.1	35.3	200.0
Indexation (at 10%) to operational date: 1.4.91			
1988/89	7.5	3.5	20.0
	82.6	38.8	220.0
1989/90	8.3	3.9	22.0
	90.9	42.7	242.0
1990/91	9.1	4.3	24.2
	100.0	47.0	266.2
Operational years:			
1991/92	10.0	4.7	26.6
	110.0	51.7	292.8
1992/93	11.0	5.2	29.3
	121.0	56.9	322.1
1993/94	12.1	5.7	32.2
	133.1	62.6	354.3
1994/95	13.3	6.3	35.4
	146.4	68.9	389.7

Notes:
1. 'Pre-Operational' payroll taken into development phase 60,000.
2. General Overheads:

Heating, Ventilation and General Maintenance	56.0
Rates	50.0
Other General Administrative Overheads	94.0
	200.0

Appendix 'D': promotional expenditure

	Pre-Operational	1st year	Units RM000s All following years
(Per report 1987)	50.0	93.0	61.0
Add for inflation:			
1988/89	5.0	9.3	6.1
	55.0	102.3	67.1
1989/90	5.5	10.2	6.7
	60.5	112.5	73.8
1990/91		11.3	7.4
1991/92			8.1
			89.3
1992/93			8.9
			98.2
1993/94			9.8
			108.0

Conclusion: key points for review

Bearing in mind the project funding requirement, and its obvious high dependency for success on the estimated throughput of visitors it would be essential to undertake a detailed check of data in the TOURISM fact sheets that could be obtained from the Malaysian Promotion of Tourism Board. Questions to ask would include:

- How many visitors come to KL each year? and are they interested in this type of educational and historic project?
- Are there any other competitive attractions?
- How does the project entry price compare with visitor spending power?
- What about the logistics of getting 500,000 people through the centre in a year?
- Does the Trust Board have the necessary management and technical skills to see through a project of this size?
- Do they have the necessary marketing skills to ensure good promotion of the centre?

There are many questions to be answered before we can be sure of the top line in our projection.

The cash flow will come from the key variables of entry price times visitor numbers. Financial support will be difficult to obtain for this project as payback of the loans will only come from positive cash flow!

From the two case studies we can draw a number of conclusions.

Often these types of project will test cash forecasting skills to the full as frequently, with project finance, it is very difficult to verify the projections. It is a key issue to confirm as best we can the likely level of cash inflow streams as it is from these that costs must be serviced and the Bank's interest charges met. To help overcome business cash flow risks a good margin of safety should be sought, both in terms of the fall-back in income stream and cash flow margins.

LONGER TERM FORECASTING

As we have seen the monthly cash forecasts tend to deal with the shorter term view. Longer term cash forecasting is linked more directly to the strategic plans of the business.

A successful corporate manager must be able to analyse, identify and understand the company's specific vulnerability and positioning within the cycles to appreciate the cash flow needs and suggest the correct financial structure. Three key periods can be identified in a company's life.

The growth period:

- Competitors enter
- Good acquisitions climate
- Under-capacity
- High profits
- Danger of over-trading
- Scramble for distribution network

In this phase it is important to build and maintain market share. Good marketing becomes imperative. Depending on market share, basic cash flow could be positive and financing decisions should be taken in the light of cash generation.

Should the growth period be too rapid however there would be a constant over-trading risk whereby any finance would be of a residual and ever-growing nature with the corporate needing to fund overall cash deficits.

The maturity period:

- Some over-capacity
- Difficult to increase market share
- Price competition
- Falling prices
- Lower margins
- Difficult to sell companies

In this period financial discipline becomes critical in all areas: particularly cost control, overheads, price, credit control. The overall strategy is to endeavour to maintain market share with a possible thought towards repositioning and diversification. Cash flow could still be negative depending on the particular industry or at best marginally positive.

The decline period:

- Substantial over-capacity
- Fewer competitors
- Falling prices and margins
- Numerous exits
- No growth potential
- Takeover possibility

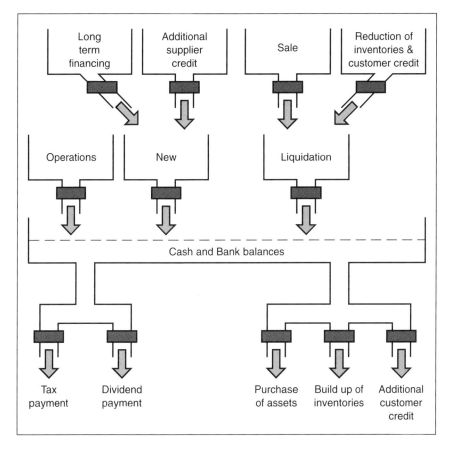

Fig 4.2 The Cash Tank

In this period survival becomes key. The strategy now focusses on terminating, diversifying and repositioning. The timing of the exit becomes crucial as regulatory and social issues have to be considered, e.g. redundancies, government action, etc.

THE CASH TANK

The format for this type of longer term forecast can vary enormously, however a useful way to commence our forecast is to use the **cash tank method.** The concept originated in the United States and involves thinking of cash as a precious liquid stored in the cash tank. The tank is fitted, as can be seen from the diagram, with inlet and outlet pipes. The level of fluid can therefore be controlled by increasing inflows or by reducing outflows or by various combinations.

PREPARING A FORECAST USING FRS 1 AND A COMPUTERISED SPREADSHEET

The next step in our long term forecasting is to move from the conceptual framework of the cash tank to preparing the forecast document. As mentioned before the options for setting this out vary, but I think a good idea is to follow the new cash statement format (FRS 1).

Let us examine the cash flow statements for the soft drinks manufacturers JN Nichols (Vimto) plc, who are a publicly quoted company manufacturing a range of soft drink products for both the carbonated and still drinks market (see pp. 155 and 156 for data).

To begin our forecast we start by focussing on the 'Notes to the cash flow statement'. It is simply a question of working down the document and forecasting operating profit, depreciation, movements in stock, debtors, creditors etc.

In order to project the operating profit we will need to look at the relationship between this and our likely projected sales figure. If we see, for example, ten per cent sales growth in the next year, and we calculate the relationship of operating profit to sales at 15% and 15.9%, then on forecast sales of £52,752,000 we would expect a profit of say £8,387,000 – provided the ratios move in a linear relationship.

After forecasting movements in the working assets, we will achieve a figure for net cash flow from continuing operating activities. This figure is then carried forward to the opening line of our cash flow statement. Next we work down the statement forecasting interest, dividends, tax, purchases/sales of assets and finally arrive at our projected net cash flow. In Nichols case, based on past trends, it should be positive. From this projection, if we were cash negative, we would need to consider **how we are going to finance this shortfall.**

TO SUMMARISE:

Cash forecasting is essential to ensure the success of the project or the survival of the corporate and both short term monthly forecasts and longer term annual forecasts are recommended to keep our focus firmly on the CASH!

This chapter has revolved around the essential aspects of cash forecasting:

- we developed a cash flow worksheet;
- and then went on to look in detail at two case studies featuring cash forecasting;
- sensitivity issues were discussed and longer term cash forecasting reviewed using, to begin with the cash-tank method, and then computerised spreadsheets.

5

CASH FLOW – CRISIS!

A cash flow crisis will often be followed by corporate failure. There have been many attempts to develop business models that can predict corporate failure. So let us begin this chapter with a review of corporate failure prediction, and an examination of failed companies after the event.

Certain characteristics tend to be displayed, both financial and non-financial, which differentiate failed from surviving companies. By testing these failure signals on existing companies, it is hoped that potential failures can be identified before the problems become too extreme to allow any type of turnaround.

There are two methods of predicting corporate failure:

- financial analysis methods;
- business risk (non-financial) methods.

The first method is a more analytical approach primarily using ratios to observe trends within the company. The second method is a more subjective approach involving looking for certain business risk danger signals which have been identified as common characteristics in failed companies.

FINANCIAL ANALYSIS METHODS

This approach assumes that as a company moves along its failure path, its financial ratios will reflect its deteriorating position. Successive financial statements of failed companies have been analysed, usually up to at least five years before failure.

Two types of studies have been undertaken:

- univariate studies – the purpose of these is to find the best single ratio to predict corporate failure;

- multivariate studies or multi-discriminate analysis (MDA) – the inter-relationships between ratios are assumed to have more predictive ability than the ratios themselves.

Univariate analysis

Probably the best known researcher in this field is Beaver who was interested in the relative predictability of current and long term ratios. Beaver studied a variety of long term and current ratios and found the best single predictor to be the **cash flow** ratio:

$$\frac{\text{Cash flow}}{\text{Total Debt}}$$

followed by:
$$\frac{\text{Net Income}}{\text{Total Debt}}$$

and
$$\frac{\text{Total Debt}}{\text{Total Assets}}$$

He also found that the share price is a useful indicator of the company's health. Share prices were seen to suffer abnormal losses *prior* to a deterioration of the financial ratios.

Univariate analysis, however, has disadvantages. These include:

- it is probably too simplistic, meaning that it is very easy to draw the wrong conclusion;
- it is vulnerable to different accounting conventions.

Multi-discriminate Analysis (MDA)

To begin with a definition: 'MDA is a statistical technique used to classify an observation into one of several groupings dependent upon the observation's individual characteristics.' (Altman 1968.)

Data is collected from the classified groups (the dependent variable is qualitative:– insolvent and surviving companies.) MDA attempts to derive a linear combination of these characteristics which best discriminates between the groups.

Altman

Probably the first and most widely known developer of MDA techniques, Professor Altman, published 'The Z Score Model' in 1968, as a predictor of corporate failure.

His work was based on 33 insolvent and 33 solvent companies. The effect of size on ratios was eliminated by excluding companies with very large or very small total assets. He found that by using five ratios he was able to predict 72% of failures two years before insolvency using the following linear equation:

$$z = 0.012\ x1 + 0.014\ x2 + 0.033\ x3 + 0.006\ x4 + 0.010\ x5$$

$$x1 = \frac{\text{Working Capital}}{\text{Total Assets}}$$

$$x2 = \frac{\text{Retained Earnings}}{\text{Total Assets}}$$

$$x3 = \frac{\text{D B I T}}{\text{Total Assets}}$$

$$x4 = \frac{\text{Market Capitalisation}}{\text{Total Debts}}$$

$$x5 = \frac{\text{Sales}}{\text{Total Assets}}$$

Altman found that companies with a Z score of less than 1.8 would fail and over 3.0 would survive. The predictive ability of the model was as follows:

One year prior to failure   –   95% correctly classified
Two years prior to failure   –   72% correctly classified
Three years prior to failure   –   48% correctly classified
Four years prior to failure   –   30% correctly classified
Five years prior to failure   –   30% correctly classified

So the most serious change in the majority of ratios occurred between two and three years prior to failure.

Criticisms of the model

There have been a number of criticisms of the Z Score Model. These include:

- beyond two years prior to failure, the model has a poorer predictive ability than a random chance model – 50:50;
- the model is based on only one small sample, therefore it is limited in depth. Furthermore the sample was drawn from manufacturing based companies;
- it does not eliminate all the problems related to ratios: for example different accounting procedures create problems. It is more objective however than univariate analysis and statistically more significant.

Following these criticisms Altman, together with Haldeman and Narayanan, improved on this first model and in 1977 published 'Zeta Analysis: a new model to identify bankruptcy risk of corporations.' It is based on seven ratios instead of five and on two samples of companies consisting of 53 failed companies and 58 surviving companies matched by industry and year of data. Over 90% were classified correctly one year prior to failure and 70% accuracy was achieved for up to five years before failure. In this Zeta model, the company's size was taken into account as measured by its total assets, and debt service was also included. The Zeta Model is said to be more accurate in predicting failure, but the basic problems of which ratios to select remain. Also the data being used is by its very nature historic.

Other models of MDA

Taffler

Possibly the most commercially successful Z score model has been developed by Richard Taffler (1977). He established a service called Performance Analysis Services and claims virtually 100% success in predicting insolvency. Banks have been amongst those using this service. He does not publish complete information and uses one model for public quoted companies and one for private companies.

Taffler's Equation (where C = Taffler's co-efficient)

Z = C + C X profitability
+ C X working capital position

+ C X gearing
+ C X liquidity

$$\text{Profitability} = \frac{\text{Profit before tax}}{\text{Current Liabilities}}$$

$$\text{Working capital position} = \frac{\text{Current Assets}}{\text{Total Liabilities}}$$

$$\text{Gearing} = \frac{\text{Current Liabilities}}{\text{Total Assets}}$$

Liquidity = 'no credit' interval =

Cash + marketable securities – current liabilities

It is noticeable that a difference in Taffler's formula is the exclusion of market capitalisation.

Bathory

Bathory undertook a survey of 350 companies and concluded that it was relatively easy to use a financial model to predict corporate failure. His results were published in early 1985. He wanted to simplify the MDA techniques and his formula takes account of five financial flows that contribute to insolvency.

1) Current Debt Serviceability

$$\frac{\text{Gross cash flow}}{\text{Current Debt}}$$

2) Actual Profitability

$$\frac{\text{Profit before tax}}{\text{Capital Employed}}$$

3) Capital Adequacy

$$\frac{\text{Equity}}{\text{Current Liabilities}}$$

4) Cumulative profitability

$$\frac{\text{Tangible Net Worth}}{\text{Total Liabilities}}$$

5) Liquidity

$$\frac{\text{Working Capital}}{\text{Total Assets}}$$

These ratios are added together and divided by five and then a constant multiple is used to arrive at a final score. These scores are then monitored over a period of years looking for deterioration.

Uses of Z scores

Z scores may be used as an index of financial vulnerability, but they must be interpreted with caution. Z scores are most useful when they are compared over successive accounting periods and a steady decline in Z scores would suggest a higher probability of failure. It is probably most accurate to say that all companies with Z scores less than the cut-off point *could* have possible future problems and require further examination.

MDA models do not replace existing evaluation procedures that generally require a skilled analyst. However Z scores can be used as a screening device and so direct attention to those companies in need of further analysis. Z scores also ignore management reactions to financial distress signals and early turnaround actions, due to the historic nature of the scores.

This method of predicting corporate failure relies on the published and internal figures of the organisation being correct but such data is often out-of-date. The business risk method seeks to take a view on the organisation as a whole to identify problem areas, and so form an opinion on the likelihood of failure.

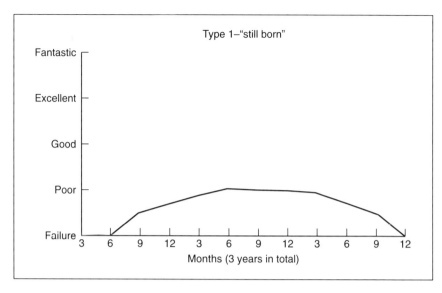

Fig 5.1 Argenti – 3 Failure Trajectories: Type 1

- Doomed from the start??
- Invariably lack of management skills
- Little active outside advice or involvement of bank
- Budgets/cash flows/sensitivity tests are a must to ascertain the chances of success

Fig 5.2 Type 1

THE BUSINESS RISK METHOD

This approach involves the identification of 'danger signals' in respect of the operations and general condition of the organisation. These 'danger signals' will have been identified as characteristics of failed companies – some justified and some more frivolous and possibly equally likely to be seen in successful companies. An endless list of these so called 'danger signals' can be made, the majority of which have little foundation: for example, the 'fountain in the forecourt' or the new flagpoles outside the office.

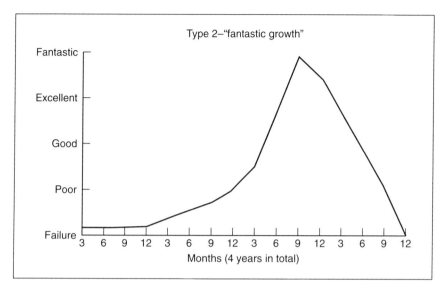

Fig 5.3   Argenti – 3 Failure Trajectories: Type 2

- Can it be rescued at peak?
- One man rule must eventually fail?
- Bottle the Genie?
- Make additions to the Board?
- More bank involvement i.e. cash flow controls

Fig 5.4   Type 2

Argenti A score

Professor John Argenti (1976) has simplified the failure process into three different types. The approach is called 'The Company Health Index.' Each potential failure can be classified as one of the three types:

Type 1 – 'Stillborn' – typically a one-person business (Figs 5.1 and 5.2)
Type 2 – Dynamic Company (Figs 5.3 and 5.4)
Type 3 – Mature Company (Figs 5.5 and 5.6)

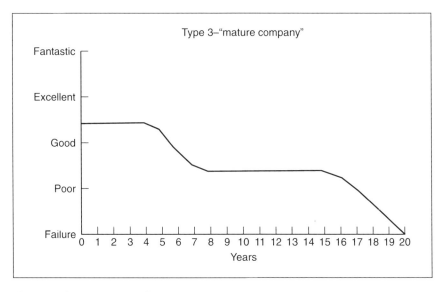

Fig 5.5 Argenti – 3 Failure Trajectories: Type 3

- A very different problem
- Cure is possible at many different points on the trajectory
- Don't remain waterlogged
- New management?
- Capital restructure?
- Plan disposals?

Fig 5.6 Type 3

Each type is easily identified by its characteristics and is potentially on a failure path. Unless rectifying action is taken, the following sequence, resulting in failure, describes the process.

Management

1. *The balance of the board* – is the chairman and chief executive one person? Is it a one-man company? Does the management have a wide range of skills?

2. *Function of the board* – is there collective decision making? Be suspicious of a single leader because there is a limit to what that one person can do. A well run company will thrive on collective decisions and collective responsibility.

3. *Middle management support* – if there is a lack of middle management it is hard to see how decisions can be implemented.

Accountancy systems

- if the **accounting system** is inadequate, proper and corrective decisions cannot be made. Progress cannot be monitored if management has no information on which to work;
- **creative accounting** is almost invariably associated with corporate failure. It is seen, for example, in the revaluing of assets, changes in the bases of stock valuations and in expenditure being carried forward. Creative accounting improves profits and liquidity ratios, but remember that profit is merely an opinion whilst cash is fact;
- **payments to creditors and collections from debtors** – a successful company will demonstrate a reasonably steady pattern. As a company moves towards failure, this pattern will begin to deteriorate since the company will not release cash in the same regular way as before. The easiest debts to collect will be pressed for and difficult ones may be ignored. This symptom occurs late on the failure path.

With one or more of these defects firmly entrenched in the company's constitution it is only a matter of time before *The Monumental Mistake* is made and leads to its ultimate failure. Argenti says that the Mistake will almost certainly be one of the following:

1. *Overtrading* – This is probably the most common mistake and occurs when the selling exuberance of the company reaches the level where sales turnover is growing faster than profits. If this continues the company will become illiquid.
2. *Overgearing* – This occurs when the company's gearing is allowed to rise to such a level that even the normal day-to-day fluctuations in the business are a threat to its survival. If this is coupled with say a recessionary down-turn the company will no longer be able to service its debts.

3. *The Too-Big Project* – The company recognises that its existing lines of business are experiencing long term difficulties, and it therefore embarks on a new and ambitious project in the hope that it will enable the company to take an enormous leap back onto a path of growth. Everything will go into this project and when delays occur, as they almost seem bound to, costs escalate and cash will be consumed at a tremendous rate. The classic example is Rolls Royce and the RB211 engine.

Note Sir Kenneth Cork's Golden Rule:

Never undertake a development, the cost of which you cannot write-off and still remain in existence.

Once one of these Monumental Mistakes has been made, the financial ratios will begin to deteriorate sharply. The management will probably attempt to conceal reality with creative accounting, for example by inflating stock value.

Argenti has designed a scoring system called the 'A' score, to highlight these potentially weak companies. The technique is illustrated as follows:

CAUSES OF BUSINESS FAILURE: THE 'A' SCORE CHECKLIST

DEFECTS	
Autocratic chief executive	8
Chairman and chief executive combines	4
Passive board	2
Unbalanced skills, especially over-technical	2
Weak finance director	2
Poor management depth below board level	1
No budgetary control	3
No cash flow plans, or no cash flow updating	3
No reliable costing system	3
Poor response to change, lack of awareness of business environment	15
TOTAL FOR DEFECTS	43
Danger marks for Defects	10

MISTAKES

High debt gearing	15
Overtrading (inadequate equity base)	15
Big project in relation to business size	15
TOTAL FOR MISTAKES	45
Danger mark for mistakes	15

SYMPTOMS

Financial signs, e.g. Z-score warning signs	4
Creative accounting, especially changes to previous policy resulting in increased stock values, lower depreciation, and capitalisation of R & D or repairs/maintenance	4
Non-financial signs, including deterioration in product quality/service, premises and morale	3
Terminal signs	1
TOTAL FOR SYMPTOMS	12
TOTAL OVERALL MAXIMUM POSSIBLE	100
DANGER MARK OVERALL	**25**

We have shown how Argenti's three profiles can help us identify the different types of company and how they can fail. The case study discussed below demonstrates clearly the second of Argenti's profiles – where a pattern of rapidly expanding sales accompanied by negative cash flow often leads to rapid business failure.

The business in question, the Nor Western Group Ltd, began with an innovative idea from its entrepreneur founder Mr PR Archer. He decided to manufacture a cheap alternative to the expensive solarium, capitalising on the potentially huge market of those seeking the sense of fitness and well-being derived from looking sun-bronzed, without having to pay too much for it.

He formed a group of companies under the name Nor Western Group Ltd.

CASE STUDY: NOR WESTERN GROUP LTD

Background

Mr Archer was experiencing some difficulties with his first bank in March 19X3 and decided to approach another banker who he hoped would have a more liberal attitude to expansion of sales. He called at the B branch of another bank to discuss matters with the branch manager. The date was April 19X3. The bank manager minuted the following:

Archer's request was for increased facilities on Bertonia Promotions Ltd; to match facilities on Trog Sheet Metal and to grant a facility on a new company, Trevision Ltd.

. . . **Bertonia** commenced trading on the 17th May 19X2 and the majority shareholder is PR Archer who guarantees the account to £15,000. There is also a company mortgage debenture charge. Whilst at first sight the company appears to be a sun-bed manufacturer, a truer definition would be a company which identifies markets with a demand for a product and fulfils that demand in the promoting or manufacturing of any items . . .

. . . figures prepared are on sun-bed sales and don't include sales of exercise bicycles and sports clothing . . . sales are received through advertising, from agents and from in-store promotional displays . . .

. . . we are asked for an overdraft of £25,000 (an increase of £10,000) to assist with office refurbishment and to allow expansion at a sensible rate for the business . . . The sun-bed product is extremely good; simple in design and very cheap at £73 . . .

. . . against a draft balance sheet the request is not out of line . . .

. . . whilst on the surface Mr Archer is very abrasive and sharp, the steady growth of the business has been excellent, the present state healthy and future potential looks good . . .

. . .**Trog Sheet Metal** manufacture the sun-beds for Bertonia and also carry out metal fabrication work (30%) . . .

. . . We are asked to match the facility at £25,000 . . . draft figures indicate a surplus around £25,000. Security will be a charge on the lease plus a guarantee . . .

. . . **Trevision** has been formed to assemble, finish off and package the sun-beds . . .

. . . initial capital is £10,000 and we have been asked for £25,000 . . .

The bank manager agreed to the requested facilities and the bank accounts were opened at B branch in May 19X3.

Later:

The first involvement of the bank's regional office was in February 19X4. The B branch manager telephoned to explain that Mr Archer was now requesting facilities of £500,000 across the group of companies and could they help him handle this request. The Branch Manager followed up his call by a letter explaining:

. . . the companies are currently experiencing temporary cash flow problems. The growth in 19X3 has been fast and whilst we would have hoped for some period of consolidation the directors would appear to want to continue with their policies of expansion. It is therefore essential to mark suitable facilities sufficient for this expansion . . . three further companies have been added to the group. These are:

Queenway Ltd, with facilities of £2,000, who will deal with the sale of toy cars imported from the Far East; **Warnok** – electro platers, with facilities of £35,000. This company was acquired in 19X3 to carry out plating for cosmetic jewellery; and **Damby Cars Ltd** who have spent two years developing a three wheel car; they bank at another branch . . .

The Regional Office Corporate manager reviewed the summary of financial information provided and noticed the following:

- the bank balances in many cases were in excess of the bank account limits;
- Damby facilities were not known;
- the latest accounts were all in draft form only and not audited, also they were for varying periods;
- Bertonia were the main selling company with sales of £1.46 million. Trevision had sales of £566,000. However as Trevision were assemblers and packagers it was unclear whether these were actual sales or just intercompany movements;
- it was also unclear whether the stated profits and net worth could be relied upon from draft figures;
- the strength and reliance of Archer's guarantee also had to be questioned.

A corporate call was made to Mr Archer's premises. These were very attractively fitted out with a product display area and also a sales training conference room.

Mr Archer's initial attitude was hostile and he could not accept the need for further explanation when he had already given details to his Branch Manager.

SUMMARY OF FINANCIAL INFORMATION
ACCOMPANYING REPORT OF FEBRUARY 19X4

Company	Bank Balance	Limit	Latest A/cs	Sales	Net Profit Before Tax	Net Worth
Bertonia	£31,379 dr	30,000	Draft (9 months) to 31.12.X3	1.46m	193K	217K
Trog	£72,737 dr	25,000	Draft (4 months) to 31.12.X3	272K	97K	241K
Trevision	£24,763 dr	25,000	Draft (8 months) to 31.12.X3	566K	3K	4K
Queenway	£6,930 dr	2,000	–	–	–	–
Warnok	£28,157 dr	35,000	Draft (3 months) to 31.12.X3	7K	(4K)	24K
Damby	Not known		Draft (9 months) to 31.12.X3	23K	(32K)	25K

Security: (i) Archer guarantees Bertonia, Trevision and Queenway
(ii) Debenture charges on Bertonia, Trog, Trevision, Warnok

However he agreed (after a while) that the amount £500,000 was significant and he would produce, with the help of his accountant, further information:

- Nor Western Group projections
  - profit budget to 31.12.X4
  - balance sheet at 31.12.X4
  - cash flow to 31.12.X4
- Nor Western Ltd and subsidiaries revised draft balance sheet at 31.12.X3
- Summary of stock as at 31.12.X3
- Debtors as at 31.12.X3 with age analysis
- Summary of fixed assets at 31.12.X3

The profit budget illustrates an expected sales turnover of £16 million resulting in a gross profit at 38.5% of £6.2 million and after deduction of overhead expenses a projected profit before taxation of £4.8 million.

PROJECTED TRADING AND PROFIT AND LOSS ACCOUNT
FOR THE YEAR TO 31ST DECEMBER 19X4

	£000's	£000's
Turnover		16,075
Deduct Cost of Sales:		
Direct Labour and Materials	4,879	
Commission Taken by Retail Outlets	3,255	
Commission Taken by Selling Agents	1,306	
Advertising	440	9,880
Gross Profit for the Year (38.5%)		6,195
Deduct Overhead Expenses:		
Administration Expenses	693	
Establishment Charges	198	
Indirect Selling Costs, including Exhibitions	167	
Financial and Professional Expenses	29	
Depreciation and Write off of Research and Development	208	1,295
		4,900
Deduct Interest Payable:		
Bank Interest	28	
Hire Purchase Interest	16	44
Projected Profit on Ordinary Activities for the Year		4,856
Deduct Taxation (estimated)		2,550
Retained Profit for the Year		2,306
Retained Profits, brought forward		484
Retained Profits, carried forward		£2,790

The retained profit of £2.8 million is carried forward into the projected balance sheet as at 31st of December 19X4. Readers will note fixed assets total 578 thousand with total current assets of £5.9 million consisting mainly of trade debtors at £4 million. The net worth of the group of companies on a consolidated basis is shown at £2.8 million in the table below.

PROJECTED BALANCE SHEET AS AT 31ST DECEMBER 19X4

	£000's	£000's
FIXED ASSETS		
Tangible Assets (net of hire purchase)		553
Research and Development		25
		578
CURRENT ASSETS		
Stock and Work in Progress	320	
Trade Debtors	4,040	
Cash at Bank	1,589	
	£5,949	
CURRENT LIABILITIES		
Trade Creditors and Accruals	1,074	
Directors' Current Accounts	109	
Corporation Tax	2,550	
	£3,733	
NET CURRENT ASSETS		2,216
		£2,794
FINANCED BY:		
SHARE CAPITAL		4
RESERVES, including Minority Interests		2,790
		£2,794

PROJECTED CASH FLOW FOR THE PERIOD 1 MARCH 19X4
TO 31 DECEMBER 19X4

In summary:	TOTAL £000s
Gross receipts	13,550.41
Deduct stores commission taken at source	2,657.22
	10,893.19
Direct costs	
Materials and labour	5,261.96
Agents commission	1,208.90
Advertising and promotional expenses	400.00
Indirect costs	
Administration expenses	536.27
Selling and distribution costs	163.48
Establishment costs	170.46
Legal and professional fees	20.70
Funding costs	28.50
H.M. Customs Excise VAT	748.38
Capital expenditure	
Outright purchase	524.05
Hire purchase – Deposits	23.40
– Repayments	67.73
	9,153.83
Cash surplus/(Deficiency) for the month	1,739.36
Bank balance, brought forward	(150.00)
Bank balance, carried forward	1,589.36

Also forwarded to the bank was a revised draft Balance Sheet as at the end of 19X3 which showed fixed assets of £232,000 and current assets of £892,000 and current liabilities of £636,000.

The resultant net worth was stated at £488,000.

**N W GROUP LIMITED AND SUBSIDIARY COMPANIES REVISED
DRAFT BALANCE SHEET AS AT 31ST DECEMBER 19X3**

	£000's	£000's
FIXED ASSETS		
Tangible Assets (net of Hire Purchase)		182
Research and Development		50
		232
CURRENT ASSETS		
Stock and Work in Progress	324	
Trade Debtors	568	
	892	
CURRENT LIABILITIES		
Bank Overdraft	113	
Trade Creditors and Accruals	514	
Directors Current Accounts	9	
	636	
NET CURRENT ASSETS		256
		488
FINANCED BY:		
SHARE CAPITAL		4
RESERVES		426
		430
MINORITY SHAREHOLDERS		58
		488

A more detailed analysis of some of the assets was also provided:

DEBTOR SUMMARY 31.12.X3

Total £504,567

Current	:	£325,366
1 Month	:	£152,603
2 Month	:	£19,083
Old	:	£7,515
TOTAL		£504,567

This schedule shows a domination of current debtors which is of course a good point and the remaining debtors are recent in terms of days outstanding.

STOCK & WORK IN PROGRESS 31.12.X3

	Stock	*WIP*
Bertonia	176,896	
Trog	9,959	54,840
Trevision	68,765	
Warnok	3,346	
Damby	10,000	
	268,966	54,840
TOTAL	£323,806	

Most of the stock is held by the main company – Bertonia – with Trog manufacturing and therefore carrying a WIP figure.

The fixed asset schedule shows significant amounts of plant and machinery and motor vehicles.

The Branch Manager put in a formal request for £500,000 total overdraft facilities which he thought would fit the expansion plans of Mr Archer's businesses.

This application was reviewed at the Regional Office but the request was thought too much. The Director at Regional Office **agreed £350,000** as a facility across the whole Group and returned the application to the Branch Manager.

FIXED ASSET SUMMARY   31.12.X3

Freehold property	54,000
Lease & improvements	9,909
Fixtures and fittings	25,411
Office equipment	19,139
Plant and Machinery	48,422
Motor Vehicles	99,751
	£256,632

During the next five months to August X4 cash flow continued to be very erratic and there were frequent referrals of excess on the group to the bank's Regional Office (RO).

By August the RO Director's patience was wearing thin and he asked the Corporate Manager to re-visit the business premises. He refused based on the fact that he hadn't supported the advance in the first place and thought there would be little to be gained by making a return visit to Archer.

After consultation it was agreed by all parties to commission a report by an independent firm of accountants, to endeavour to find out the exact current position across the Group and the way forward in terms of the cash flow requirements and future business viability.

The following is extracted from the accountants' report:

ACCOUNTANTS' REPORT – 22.8.X4

1 BUSINESS

1.1 Nor Western Ltd, which acts as the group holding company, was incorporated on 28 October 19X3 and progressively acquired the following group companies:

Bertonia Promotions Limited	– markets all group products other than those manufactured by Trog (see below). Offices in leasehold premises at Edward Street, Bolton.
Trog Sheet Metal Products Limited	– manufacturer with 90% of turnover inter-group, and 10%

	sales to third parties. Leasehold premises are situated at Church Street, Bolton.
Trevision Limited	– assembles components manufactured by Trog from leasehold premises at Williamson, Bolton. Sales are entirely inter-group.
Damby Cars Limited	– manufacturer of the three wheeled 'Damby' micro motor car from leasehold premises at Brighton Street, Bolton.
Warnok Electro Plating Limited	– non trading
Queenway Limited	– non trading

1.2   The Group's products and selling lines consist of:

Bertonia UVA sunbeds and Bertafit cycles and rowing machines	– manufactured by Trog, assembled by Trevision and sold by Bertonia. Bertonia products represented 92% of the group's turnover for the three months to 30 June 19X4.
Damby motor cars and children's pedal cars	– the Damby is designed to fill the gap between the small car and the moped/scooter market. Due to various problems with supplies etc, there were no sales in the three months to 30 June 19X4.
Hotel Holiday Breaks	– a holiday voucher scheme utilising the available space in large hotel chains. No sales in the three months.
Trog fabricated products	– manufactured by Trog and sold direct to third parties. Six and a

	half per cent of the group's turnover for the three months to 30 June 19X4.
Sundry bought in products	– toy dodgem cars, luggage etc. There were very few sales of these products in the three months to 30 June 19X4.
Sunmax	– a PVC based film which minimises the toxic effects of over-exposure to the sun particularly by acting as a filter.

1.3 NOR group's customers are mainly established public companies of substance and the group is not reliant on any one customer. Suppliers are numerous with different sources being used for most types of material or component purchased. We have been told that because of arrears in the settlement of suppliers' accounts NOR is currently experiencing difficulty in obtaining supplies on credit.

1.4 The authorised share capital of NOR, as stated in its Memorandum of Association, is £12,000 dividend into 12,000 ordinary shares of £1 each. The allocated, called-up and fully paid share capital is £4,000 and is held beneficially by Mr Archer. We have been told that it is intended to increase the allotted share capital to £500,000 by the capitalisation of reserves.

1.5 The group acquired a Sirius 1 computer in 19X3 and is progressively computerising the whole of its accounting records.

We set out below our understanding of the accounting records of each of the trading companies within the group:

(a) Bertonia

The nominal and purchase ledgers and pay-roll records were computerised in July 19X3 and the sales ledger in November 19X3. The cash book is recorded manually. There are no perpetual stock records but stocks are physically counted every quarter.

(b) Trog

All records are presently handwritten. There are no control accounts in the sales and purchase ledgers and these were reconciled by Messrs

Dutton Moore at the end of March and June 19X4. The company does not maintain a nominal ledger and accounts are prepared from the books of prime entry by Messrs Dutton Moore. Kardex stock records is currently underway. At present, however, there are no perpetual stock records.

(c) Trevision

Sales, purchases and nominal ledgers were computerised from 1 April 19X4. There are no perpetual stock records but stocks are physically counted every quarter.

The directors are currently considering the acquisition of a larger computer, possibly an IBM 36.

1.6 Despite the absence of perpetual stock records, we are informed that the directors and senior employees are continually monitoring stock levels.

1.7 In the time available we have not reviewed the Memorandum and Articles of Association of each of the group companies.

1.8 We have been told that Bertonia has a products liability insurance policy giving cover of £1m.

The accountants then went on to examine the trading results and concluded that profits were being earned although they did not verify the stock holdings.

2 TRADING RESULTS

2.1 We set out below the audited consolidated trading results of NOR for the period to 31 March 19X4 and the consolidated management accounts for the three months to 30 June 19X4. The consolidated accounts to 31 March 19X4 are derived from the audit accounts of NOR and its subsidiaries and are before the elimination of profits pre-acquisition to NOR. The accounts of the subsidiaries are in respect of the following periods:

Bertonia	–	year to 31 March 19X4
Trog	–	1 September 19X3 to 31 March 19X4
Trevision	–	9 May 19X3 to 31 March 19X4
Damby	–	– year ended 31 March 19X4
Warnok	–	1 October 19X3 to 31 March 19X4
Queenway	–	1 February 19X4 to 31 March 19X4

These have been derived from the audited accounts for the period ended 31 March 19X4 and from the books and records of NOR and its subsidiaries for the period 1 April to 30 June 19X4. As regards the audited accounts the audit report of NOR included the following qualifications:

(a) the auditors were appointed after the year end and were unable, therefore, to attend the stocktakes.
(b) reference was made to a note in the audit report for Damby that the accounts had been prepared on a going concern basis which assumed that the holding company and Damby's fellow subsidiaries would continue to provide support for Damby.
(c) the group's system of control is dependent upon the close involvement of the chairman and major shareholder and it was necessary for the auditors to accept assurances from the chairman when the completeness of the accounting records was not available.

	Notes	3 months to 30 June 19X4 £'000	Periods to 31 March 19X4 £'000
Sales	2.2	943	2,114
Cost of sales		343	1,080
Gross profit	2.3	600	1,034
Administration		105	250
Selling and distribution		166	323
Establishment		47	80
Finance charges		5	23
Interest payable		14	15
		337	691
Net profit		263	343
Other income	2.4	10	32
Profit before tax		273	375
Taxation	2.5	57	47
Retained profit		216	328

2.2 The increased turnover in the three months to 30 June 19X4 is said to reflect the continuing growth of the group. Sales for July 19X4 were £350,000 and we have been told that August is likely to produce a similar figure.

2.3 We have been told that the increased gross margin is due to the high proportion of sales of sunbeds from Ideal Homes and other exhibitions in the period. These beds are not only sold at up to twice the price obtained from comparable sales to stores and mail order firms but in addition the expenses of the exhibitions were incurred and charged in the accounts for the period to 31 March 19X4.

2.4 Other income for the period to 30 June 19X4 consists of regional development grants receivable and we would recommend that it would be more appropriate to credit this amount to a separate account in the balance sheet and to release it to profit and loss over the life of the related fixed assets.

2.5 Provision for corporation tax has been made at a rate of 35% on the profit for the period to 30 June 19X4. We estimate that the provision is understated by approximately £17,000. No provision for deferred taxation has been made at either date.

3.1 Stocks and work in progress

Stock records at Trog and Trevision are currently being introduced but at the 30 June 19X4 none of the group companies maintained any perpetual stock records and all stock quantities were obtained by physical counts. As we were unable to attend the physical stocktake we are unable to comment on the accuracy of the physical quantities included in the stock valuation.

The basis of valuation was reviewed and values compared to the evaluated stock sheets at 31 March 19X4. Certain lines appearing in the stocks of Trevision and Trog would, in our opinion, be best written off as incurred but we were able to conclude that these items were not of material value and their inclusion in the accounts was consistent with previous periods.

Included in the stocks of are the following bought-in items:

	Units	£
Toy dodgem sets	55,985	106,371
Luggage sets	2,324	25,684
		132,055

We have been told that whilst there does not appear to be much of a market for these items at the present time the directors are sure the items will be sold prior to Christmas 19X4 for at least their carrying values.

No adjustment has been made to the consolidated profit and loss account at either 31 March or 30 June 19X4.

3.2 Debtors

Approximately 93% of the total debtors relates to Bertonia's sales ledger. Whilst debtors represent approximately three months' sales, most are public companies. Cash received in respect of these debts has so far been in line.

Bertonia's trade debtors at 30 June 19X4 consist of the following:

	£'000	%
Binns stores	193	24
TV Times	106	13
Debenhams plc	82	10
Rackhams plc	55	7
Army & Navy plc	52	6
Fraser stores	46	6
Other (approximately 30 accounts)	272	34
	806	100

Trog trade debtors at 30 June 19X4 consist of the following:

	£'000	%
N Tucker Heating Limited	6	18
Setonway Limited	5	15
Humberside Machinery and Manufacturing Co Limited	5	15
Acomb Cranes Limited	2	6
Manville (GB) Limited	1	3
Others (approximately 20 accounts)	16	43
	34	100

We have been told that the directors have recently instructed Messrs Dunn & Bradstreet to collect all debts over two months old.

3.3 Bank overdraft (£350,000)

The NOR group companies all bank with The Bank plc at the Quay Branch where borrowing facilities have been available and are secured by debentures given by all companies within the group.

3.4 Trade and other creditors

Trade and other creditors at 30 June 19X4 may be analysed as follows:

	£'000
Trade	470
VAT – for varying periods according to company	160
PAYE and NIC – X3/4 and X4/5 according to company	109
Hire purchase	69
Sundry	49
	857

(This creditor schedule shows a significant amount of trade credit at £470,000 and also unpaid taxes totalling £269,000.)

3.5 **Taxation**

The taxation provision at 30 June 19X4 consists of:

£'000

Corporation tax for the period:
to 31 March 19X4   108

SUMMARY AND CONCLUSION

1 As requested we reviewed the various forecasts prepared and during our review it became clear that certain of the projections, particularly those relating to turnover and to the future working capital requirements, required revision. Consequently, the projections were revised.

2 We recommend that the capital base of the company be increased to better reflect the growth of the group and understand that the directors of NOR are currently considering the increasing of the issued capital to £500,000 by way of the capitalisation of reserves.

3 It is clear from the cash flow projections that the group cannot carry on trading with its reduced overdraft facility and if the facility is not increased within the next few weeks, the directors must actively seek additional finance from other sources if the group is to continue to trade. The cash flow projections prepared by NOR indicate a requirement for £500,000 until March 19X5 and thereafter £400,000 but subject to review at that time according to achievements in the period up to then.

Yours faithfully

ACCOUNTANTS

APPENDIX

NOR WESTERN LIMITED

CASH FLOW FORECAST FOR THE 9 MONTHS ENDING
31 MARCH 19X5

	19X4 *July* £	*August* £	*September* £
INCOME			
Sales	340,636	396,000	458,466
Other receipts			30,000
VAT outputs	51,095	59,400	68,770
	391,731	455,400	557,236
EXPENDITURE			
Materials	200,249	226,600	291,772
Payroll	20,000	16,000	56,660
Agents commission	17,000	18,000	20,000
Advertising and promotions	6,231	10,000	5,000
Administration	63,140	59,740	60,180
Selling and distribution	13,055	13,655	14,755
Establishment costs	21,000	21,000	21,000
Legal and professional	2,000	1,000	4,000
Capital		22,000	3,000
Hire purchase	6,495	8,195	5,195
Corporation tax			
VAT inputs	36,223	45,368	51,707
VAT payments			28,905
	385,393	441,558	562,174
MOVEMENT	6,338	13,843	(4,938)
OPENING BALANCE	(453,000)	(446,662)	(432,819)
INTEREST			(16,050)
CLOSING BALANCE	(446,662)	(432,819)	(453,807)

| | | | 19X5 | | | |
October £	November £	December £	January £	February £	March £	Total £
614,666	765,366	832,866	654,866	937,366	1,123,366	6,123,098
	75,000					105,000
92,200	114,805	124,855	98,230	140,605	168,505	918,505
706,866	955,171	957,221	753,096	1,077,971	1,291,871	7,146,563
300,000	547,933	528,951	430,801	544,176	769,551	3,840,027
61,666	61,666	30,000	30,000	30,000	35,000	340,027
20,000	20,000	25,000	16,000	18,000	55,000	209,000
25,000	40,000	30,000	60,000	80,000	50,000	306,231
67,510	61,040	62,460	63,140	63,140	63,140	563,490
14,755	15,755	15,755	13,055	13,055	13,055	126,895
21,000	21,000	21,000	21,000	21,000	21,000	189,000
6,000	10,000	4,000	2,000	2,000	2,000	33,000
20,000	15,000	36,000	32,000	50,000	61,000	239,000
7,195	7,195	7,195	6,495	6,495	6,495	60,955
				108,255		108,255
59,093	98,532	96,435	84,803	122,509	123,465	718,135
40,000	40,000	106,442	40,000			255,347
64,219	938,121	963,239	799,294	1,058,630	1,199,706	6,990,333
64,647	17,049	(6,018)	(46,198)	19,341	92,165	156,229
(454,807)	(389,160)	(372,111)	(393,553)	(439,751)	(420,410)	(453,000)
		(15,424)			(13,400)	(44,874)
(389,160)	(372,111)	(393,553)	(439,410)	(420,410)	(341,645)	(341,645)

NOR WESTERN LIMITED – APPENDIX – NOTES ON THE CASH FLOW

DEBTORS

Debts at 30 June 19X4 represented approximately three months' sales. This has been reduced gradually in the cash flow forecast to 30 days on the grounds that IPC, representing 66% of the Bertonia sales and 54% of total sales, have promised to pay within 14 days. In addition, the group now has the staff to chase debtors and ensure, as far as possible, that cash is received on time. In this context it should be noted that the majority of the group's trade is with large public companies.

OTHER INCOME

Other income consists of the sale of Warnok property and certain freehold land.

CREDITORS

Purchase creditors at 30 June represented approximately 56 days' purchases and by mid August this figure had further increased due to the reduction in the overdraft facility. The cash flow has been prepared on the basis that the number of days' credit be reduced to 45 days over the next few months.

BANK INTEREST AND BALANCES

Bank interest has been calculated at a rate of approximately 14%. The opening bank balance at 1 July 19X4 and 31 July 19X4 are the balances per the cash book and not the bank statements.

PAY-ROLL

Pay-roll in September and October includes arrears in respect of outstanding PAYE and NIC at 30 June 19X4.

RESEARCH AND DEVELOPMENT

No account has been taken in the projected profit and loss account of the write back of research and development in respect of the Damby car.

GENERAL

NOR's directors have been conservative in respect of anticipated sales and on the gross margins and expenses.

RETURNS

No specific provisions have been made for returns although the sales figures have all been heavily discounted.

NOR WESTERN LIMITED – APPENDIX – SUGGESTIONS FOR IMPROVEMENT TO THE ACCOUNTING SYSTEMS

1 Proper accounting records should be maintained for each company. This must include the recording of all transactions from receipt and control of cheques and invoices within incoming mail to the timely recording also of sales and related invoices. The immediate recording of purchase invoices to qualify for input VAT can by itself produce substantial savings.

2 We recommend that the current computerisation of the records of all group companies be expedited in order that the group might better cope with the budgeted increase in turnover and activity.

3 Prior to the computerisation of the book-keeping at Trog, the accounting records of that company should be expanded to include a nominal ledger together with purchase, sales and nominal ledger control accounts.

4 The invoicing procedure for goods despatched by Trog to Trevision should be simplified so that Trog's sales invoices are raised on despatch of the goods rather than when the goods are packed by Trevision.

5 The implementation of perpetual stock records at all companies should be continued so that physical stock checks may be compared with book stocks. This will simplify the preparation of monthly management accounts.

6 Management information in general should be improved and prepared promptly. This will improve with the continuing computerisation and the strengthened accounting team.

7 Consolidated accounts should exclude inter-company profits on stocks.

8 We recommend that management accounts be prepared at the end of September 19X4 and a comparison made with the profit projection and cash flow projection at that date.

All the above recommendations have been discussed and agreed with the directors and many of the areas requiring improvement have already been identified by the directors.

We would emphasise that the above matters came to our attention during our brief review of the management accounting systems and are not intended to include all suggestions for improvement of the systems which a special review in conjunction with the Financial Controller might identify.

Note to readers:

Please look closely at the case study cash forecast. Although it seems to fit neatly into an overall maximum requirement of £500 thousand which fits in with the request to the bank, in fact the cash flow has been manipulated by the speedier collection of debtors as illustrated in the notes to the cash flow statement.

However the bank accepted this and extended the credit line of £500 thousand.

A few weeks later there were extreme cash flow difficulties; once again together with a demand for back payment of VAT. A receiver was appointed under the bank's debenture charge.

The company broke up badly due to its many diverse interests and pressing creditors. The dividend payout on receivership was very poor and the principal narrowly avoided personal bankruptcy.

Cash flow lessons from this case study

- The cash flow needed for the manufacture of the core product – the sunbed – would be in itself a drain on any expanding company's cash resources.
- Further cash flow is needed in order that a corporate can make acquisitions such as Queenway and Warnok.
- In any development project such as Damby cars significant amounts of cash are needed to complete research and development for the car together with prototypes for regulatory testing. Further cash flow is needed to embark on any possible manufacturing of the car.
- Despite experiencing cash flow problems, Archer continued with his insatiable appetite for expansion and even when in a position of cash flow distress he tried to add two further schemes to his portfolio of companies – Hotel Holiday Breaks – a holiday voucher scheme utilising the available space in large hotel chains; and Sunmax – a PVC based film which minimises the toxic effects of over-exposure to the sun particularly through acting as a filter.
- Further cash flow was needed for the holding of stock from imports and hopefully subsequent sale of the toy dodgem cars and soft luggage sets.

In conclusion, perhaps if Archer had met someone as strong in financial controls and cash management as he himself was an undoubtedly strong salesperson then the business could have developed more sensibly and with careful cash management may have succeeded!

Product Market	Present	New
Present	Market penetration	Product development
New	Market development	Diversification

Landmarks

_____

_____

Corporate development

_____

_____

_____

Fig 5.7 Ansoff: Product Market Matrix

In the Nor Western case study, cash flow management was more or less non-existent and in fact cash flow utilised for corporate diversification can often lead to a cash crisis. This is particularly true if these developments are not planned carefully in terms of cash flow management.

CORPORATE DEVELOPMENT INTO NEW PRODUCTS AND NEW MARKETS

The most widely recognised business model for pinpointing corporate development and market positioning of products is the Ansoff – Product Market Matrix as shown above.

As the diagram shows, by placing any company's products and markets on the matrix, it is possible to consider a range of strategies available to that company. For example, one strategy would be to increase market share in existing markets – which is a relatively low-risk strategy. Alternatively it may be desirable or necessary to find new markets for existing products, or

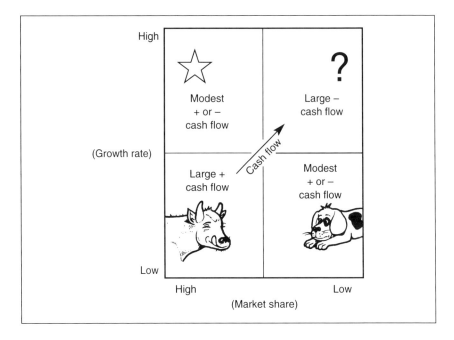

Fig 5.8 Growth/Market Share Matrix

to develop new products to sell into current markets. With adequate research this too could be a relatively low-risk strategy. The most risky strategy involves developing new products for new markets, or total diversification.

This approach can be usefully applied to businesses of all sizes, and to operating units within any business.

PINPOINTING MARKET SHARE/GROWTH AND CASH FLOW

A technique for understanding a company's likely cash flow requirements from any business or business unit has been developed by the Boston Consultancy Group. This takes into account both growth rate and market share.

The group suggested that the four quadrants of the diagram be called The Star, The Problem Child, The Cash Cow, and The Dog. Generally speaking Cash Cows, which have a high share of low growth markets, should generate healthy cash flows. Dogs can be cash traps because of their very weak competitive position, while Stars, with high growth and high market share,

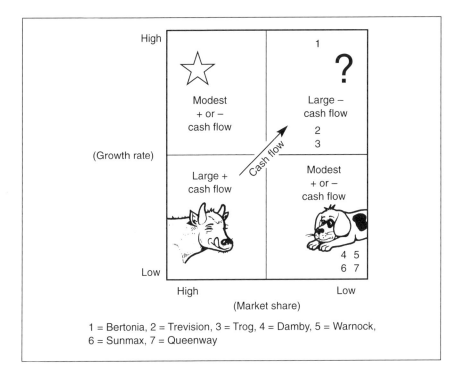

High

Modest
+ or −
cash flow

1

?

Large −
cash flow

2
3

(Growth rate)

Cash flow

Large +
cash flow

Modest
+ or −
cash flow

4 5
6 7

Low

High

Low

(Market share)

1 = Bertonia, 2 = Trevision, 3 = Trog, 4 = Damby, 5 = Warnock,
6 = Sunmax, 7 = Queenway

Fig 5.9 Nor Western Group

should yield high profits, but may need cash investment to sustain their position. The Question Mark, or Problem Child will typically need a large cash inflow to finance its growth to a position of large market share in the expanding market.

If we now return to the Nor Western case study it is possible to pinpoint the activities on this matrix across the diverse developments that Archer undertook and equally, if not more importantly, the **extreme** cash flow requirements evolving from his strategy **(or lack of it)**. This is shown in the figure above.

The BCG model also adapts itself to cash flow management of projects; for example that of a construction company where they should endeavour, if at all possible, to be in a composite cash flow positive position to help balance other projects in development stages.

Product Market	Present	New
Present	Market penetration 1	Product development 2
New	Market development	Diversification 3

Key:

1 = Salariums

2 = Sunmacs

3 = Soft luggage, Damby cars, Electro-plating,

hotel vouchers, imported toys

Fig 5.10 Nor Western Group

CONCLUSION

In this chapter we have looked at:

- predicting corporate failure;
- using multi-discriminate analysis techniques;
- using business risk techniques to predict failure;
- examining the cash flow implications of diversification;
- implementing the Ansoff matrix to pinpoint developments;
- the cash crisis case study – Nor Western;
- and finally we examined an Investigating Accountant's report and break-up issues on receivership.

6

CASH FLOW – LESSONS FROM THE USA

USING DU-PONT ANALYSIS

The US chemical manufacturer, Du-Pont, introduced many years ago a system of management control ratios for the monitoring and control of business performance. These incorporated profitability ratios and the utilisation of cash flow, within the context of asset investment and return.

Since that time ratio analysis has developed into many sophisticated formats. It is, however, worth restating Du-Pont's original formula:

RETURN ON ASSETS (ROA) =
INCOME/SALES * SALES/TOTAL ASSETS

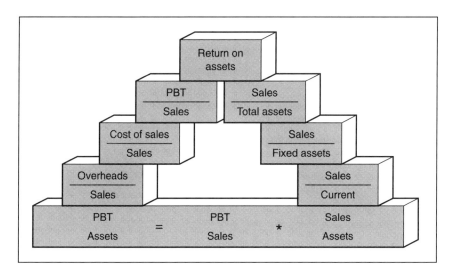

Fig 6.1   Du-Pont Pyramid of Ratios

The basic concept is illustrated in Figure 6.1.

For readers unfamiliar with Ratio analysis – please refer to the sister book in this series on ratio analysis.

The left side of the pyramid focusses on profitability ratios and the right side looks at asset utilisation. By monitoring the performance of the key ratio – ROA, a corporate can check on annual trends of return on assets and also compare its performance with corporates in similar industrial sectors.

The second use is then the ability to carry out a 'diagnostic-check'. By analysing profitability ratios down the left side of the pyramid, we can check on trading margins, while by analysing asset utilisation ratios on the right side we can check on the effective utilisation of assets.

The return on assets can be seen, therefore, to be a multiple of the profit margin on sales and the rate of asset turnover. If the overall return is improving it must be due to improved profitability, improved asset usage, or both.

A good way of monitoring ratios is to utilise a computer based financial analysis package. There are a number of such systems around to enable the corporate to undertake effective management controls.

JN NICHOLS (VIMTO) PLC

INCOME STATEMENTS

£'000	1991	1992	19XZ	19YA	19YB
TOTAL SALES	47,025	47,048	0	0	0
Cost of sales	(34,437)	(33,480)	0	0	0
GROSS PROFIT	12,588	13,568	0	0	0
Other operational costs	(5,524)	(6,084)	0	0	0
OPERATING PROFIT	7,064	7,484	0	0	0
Investment income	643	875	0	0	0
Related company income	0	0	0	0	0
Other income	0	0	0	0	0
Interest payable	0	0	0	0	0
Profit sharing	0	0	0	0	0
Exceptional items	0	0	0	0	0
PROFIT/(LOSS) BEFORE TAX	7,707	8,359	0	0	0
Tax payable	(2,536)	(2,755)	0	0	0
Deferred tax	0	0	0	0	0
Related company tax	0	0	0	0	0

PROFIT/(LOSS) AFTER TAX	5,171	5,604	0	0	0
Extraordinary items	0	0	0	0	0

PROFIT/(LOSS) AFTER EXTRAORDINARY ITEMS	5,171	5,604	0	0	0
Dividends	(1,948)	(2,154)	0	0	0

RETAINED EARNINGS/(LOSS)	3,223	3,450	0	0	0

Earnings per share (pence)	32.6	35.4	0.0	0.0	0.0
Dividend per share (pence)	12.3	13.6	0.0	0.0	0.0
Number of employees	253	254	0	0	0

JN NICHOLS (VIMTO) PLC

BALANCE SHEETS £'000	1991	1992	19XZ	19YA	19YB
Properties	2,564	2,647	0	0	0
Plant and machinery	4,337	4,789	0	0	0
Fixtures, fittings & equipment	0	0	0	0	0

TANGIBLE FIXED ASSETS	6,901	7,436	0	0	0
Intangible assets	0	0	0	0	0
Related companies	0	0	0	0	0
Other investments	0	0	0	0	0
Other fixed assets	0	0	0	0	0

FIXED ASSETS	6,901	7,436	0	0	0
Stock	2,502	2,617	0	0	0
Trade debtors	7,357	8,334	0	0	0
Short term deposits & cash	6,593	9,614	0	0	0
Other current assets	549	778	0	0	0

CURRENT ASSETS	17,001	21,343	0	0	0
Borrowings	0	0	0	0	0
Trade creditors	3,698	4,956	0	0	0
Current tax due	2,971	3,085	0	0	0
Proposed dividends	1,219	1,346	0	0	0
Other current liabilities	807	969	0	0	0

CURRENT LIABILITIES < 1 YR	8,695	10,356	0	0	0

NET CURRENT ASSETS	8,306	10,987	0	0	0

TOTAL ASSETS LESS CURRENT LIABILITIES	15,207	18,423	0	0	0
Borrowings	0	0	0	0	0
Taxation	0	0	0	0	0
Trade & other creditors	0	0	0	0	0
Provisions	235	21	0	0	0
CREDITORS > 1 YEAR	235	21	0	0	0
NET ASSETS	14,972	18,402	0	0	0
Called up share capital	3,960	3,960	0	0	0
Share premium account	671	671	0	0	0
Revaluation reserve	0	0	0	0	0
Profit & loss account	9,594	13,024	0	0	0
Other reserves	747	747	0	0	0
SHARE CAPITAL & RESERVES	14,972	18,402	0	0	0

JN NICHOLS (VIMTO) PLC

CASH FLOW STATEMENT £'000	1991	1992	19XZ	19YA	19YB
NET CASH INFLOW FROM CONTINUING OPERATING ACTIVITIES	7,070	8,781	0	0	0
NET CASH OUTFLOW FROM DISCONTINUING ACTIVITY& REORGANISATION COSTS	0	0	0	0	0
NET CASH (OUTFLOW)/ INFLOW FROM OPERATING ACTIVITIES	7,070	8,781	0	0	0
Interest received	656	820	0	0	0
Interest paid	(13)	(7)	0	0	0
Interest element of finance Lease rental payments	0	0	0	0	0
Dividend paid	(1,790)	(2,027)	0	0	0

NET CASH INFLOW/ (OUTFLOW) FROM INVESTMENT RETURNS AND SERVICING OF FINANCE	(1,147)	(1,214)	0	0	0
UK Corp. tax received/(paid)	(1,394)	(2,855)	0	0	0
Overseas tax received/(paid)	0	0	0	0	0
TAXATION RECEIVED/(PAID)	(1,394)	(2,855)	0	0	0
Purchase of tangible fixed assets	(1,449)	(1,937)	0	0	0
Sale of tangible fixed assets	496	204	0	0	0
Proceeds from divestments	0	1,102	0	0	0
Purchase of investments	0	−1040	0	0	0
Other investments	−279	−20	0	0	0
Grants received	0	0	0	0	0
NET CASH (OUTFLOW)/INFLOW FROM INVESTING ACTIVITIES	(1,232)	(1,691)	0	0	0
NET CASH (OUTFLOW)/ INFLOW BEFORE FINANCING	3,297	3,021	0	0	0
Issue of ordinary share	0	0	0	0	0
Secured loans repaid	0	0	0	0	0
Unsecured loans repaid	0	0	0	0	0
Net cash flow from capital part of finance leases	0	0	0	0	0
NET CASH (INFLOW)/ OUTFLOW FROM FINANCING	0	0	0	0	0
(DECREASE)/INCREASE IN CASH & CASH EQUIVALENTS	3,297	3,021	0	0	0
CHECK-TOTALS	3,297	3,021	0	0	0

JN NICHOLS (VIMTO) PLC

NOTES TO CASH FLOW STATEMENT

£'000	1991	1992	19XZ	19YA	19YB

1. RECONCILIATION OF OPERATING PROFIT TO NET CASH INFLOW FROM OPERATING ACTIVITIES

	1991	1992	19XZ	19YA	19YB
Operating profit	7,064	7,484	0	0	0
Depreciation charges	1,121	1,184	0	0	0
Royalties received	0	0	0	0	0
Profit received from associated undertakings	0	0	0	0	0
Loss on sale of tangible fixed assets	44	14	0	0	0
(Increase)/decrease in stocks	530	(115)	0	0	0
Decrease in debtors	(616)	(1,206)	0	0	0
Increase/(decrease) in creditors	(1,073)	1,420	0	0	0
Increase/(decrease) in provisions	0	0	0	0	0
Exchange movements	0	0	0	0	0
Other items	0	0	0	0	0
NET CASH INFLOW FROM CONTINUING OPERATING ACTIVITIES	7,070	8,781	0	0	0

JN NICHOLS (VIMTO) PLC

CASH FLOW ANALYSIS

£'000	1991	1992	19XZ	19YA	19TB
Cash flow from operations	7,070	8,781	0	0	0
Cash inflow/(outflow) from inv. returns+debt servicing	(1,147)	(1,214)	0	0	0
Tax received/(paid)	(1,394)	(2,855)	0	0	0
Cash inflow/(outflow) from investing activities	(1,232)	(1,691)	0	0	0
NET CASH INFLOW/ (OUTFLOW) BEFORE FINANCING	3,297	3,021	0	0	0

Net cash outflow/ (inflow) from financing	0	0	0	0	0
Increase/(decrease) in cash & cash equivalents	3,297	3,021	0	0	0
CHECK-TOTALS	3,297	3,021	0	0	0
CASH FLOW RATIOS:					
Cash flow interest cover	543.8	1254.2	0.0	0.0	0.0
Cash coverage ratio	6.2	7.2	0.0	0.0	0.0
Cash flow/sales (%)	15.0	18.7	0.0	0.0	0.0

JN NICHOLS (VIMTO) PLC

FINANCIAL PROFILE £'000	1991	1992	19XZ	19YA	19YB
PROFIT AND LOSS:					
Sales	47,025	47,048	0	0	0
Profit before tax	7,707	8,359	0	0	0
ASSETS AND LIABILITIES:					
Total assets	23,902	28,779	0	0	0
Current assets	17,001	21,343	0	0	0
Current liabilities	8,695	10,356	0	0	0
Capital and reserves	14,972	18,402	0	0	0
PROFITABILITY RATIOS:					
Return on total assets (%)	32.2	29.0	0.0	0.0	0.0
Gross profit margin (%)	26.8	28.8	0.0	0.0	0.0
Operating profit margin (%)	15.0	15.9	0.0	0.0	0.0
Profit before tax (%)	16.4	17.8	0.0	0.0	0.0
EFFICIENCY RATIOS:					
Asset utilisation	2.0	1.6	0.0	0.0	0.0
Sales/fixed assets	6.8	6.3	0.0	0.0	0.0
Stock turnover (days)	26.5	28.5	0.0	0.0	0.0
Trade credit taken (days)	39.2	54.0	0.0	0.0	0.0
Trade credit given (days)	57.1	64.7	0.0	0.0	0.0
Liquidity	2.0	2.1	0.0	0.0	0.0
NWA/sales (%)	13.1	12.7	0.0	0.0	0.0

JN NICHOLS (ViMTO) PLC

FINANCIAL PROFILE CONTINUED

£'000	1991	1992	19XZ	19YA	19YB
FINANCING RATIOS:					
Gearing (%)	0.0	0.0	0.0	0.0	0.0
Interest cover	7,707,000.0	8,359,000.0	0.0	0.0	0.0
Leverage (%)	59.6	56.4	0.0	0.0	0.0
EMPLOYEE RATIOS:					
Number of employees	253	254	0	0	0
Sales/employee	185.9	185.2	0.0	0.0	0.0
Profit/employee	30.5	32.9	0.0	0.0	0.0
Capital/employce	59.2	72.4	0.0	0.0	0.0
MARKET PERFORMANCE:					
Dividend per share (pence)	12.3	13.6	0.0	0.0	0.0
Earnings per share (pence)	32.6	35.4	0.0	0.0	0.0
GROWTH RATIOS:					
Actual sales	47,025	47,048	0	0	0
Sales (%)		0.0	−100.0	0.0	0.0
Profit (loss) before tax	7,707	8,359	0	0	0
(%) Increase in profit/loss (+ no.) or					
(%) Fall in profit/loss (− no.)		8.5	−100.0	0.0	0.0
Capital and reserves	14,972	18,402	0	0	0.
Capital & reserves (%)		22.9	−100.0	0.0	0.0
OTHER RATIOS:					
Break-even sales	18,234	18,063	0	0	0
Margin of safety (%)	61.2	61.6	0.0	0.0	0.0
Sustainable growth rate (%)	27.4	23.1	0.0	0.0	0.0

CASE STUDY: JN NICHOLS (VIMTO) PLC

As the tables above show, a system such as this clearly illustrates the trends over a period of time as well as giving management key information on the profitability and asset usage within the corporate. Modern computer packages also show cash generation or absorption. Nichols are quite clearly cash generators and very efficient in terms of net working asset ratios, bearing in mind they are soft drinks manufacturers. The cash flow analysis shows some very positive cash management practices.

$$G = \frac{P(1-D)\,(1+L)}{T-(P(1-D)\,(1+L))} \times 100$$

G = Sustainable growth rate
D = Dividends/profit after tax
P = Profit after tax/sales
L = Total liabilities/equity
T = Total assets/sales

Note: assumes linear movements.

Fig 6.2 Sustainable Growth Rate Formula

The sustainable growth ratio is calculated using the formula above. This ratio is not very well known. It tells us the level of sales growth that a corporate can achieve without increasing its ratio of external liabilities to net worth. It is a very useful tool in looking ahead at the likely cash requirements. If the corporate is known to be planning sales expansion ahead of its sustainable growth rate, then the gap will need to be financed in some way or another – usually by the bank. As you can see from our example, Nichols are growing at a rate they can easily sustain, and this in turn will mean even more positive cash flow.

A word of caution : as with many ratios you must use with care, the formula is based on the assumption of 'linear movements', in other words that balance sheet asset and liabilities will continue to move in line as before.

EARLY WARNING SIGNS OF BANKRUPTCY USING CASH FLOW ANALYSIS

A major study in the US by Gahlon & Vigeland in 1988 examined in depth cash flow variables between corporates and concluded that there were seven key cash flow variables. These suggested ratios capture statistically significant differences between bankrupt and non-bankrupt firms, on average, as much as five years prior to bankruptcy. These ratios and variables are strong candidates for inclusion in the 'early warning systems' that we can use for identifying potential problems.

The cornerstone of the emphasis is on past and prospective cash flows together with close scrutiny of the economic and competitive environments, managerial performance, and traditional operating and financial ratios. As noted by Malcolm Murray Jr., former president of Robert Morris Associates, 'this (emphasis on cash flow) all comes back to the fundamental premise that bank loans can be repaid only with cash.'

This narrative reports the results of a comparison of the cash flow profiles and selected ratios of a sample of companies which ultimately filed for bankruptcy with those of a sample of non-bankrupt companies. The comparison of their cash flow profiles is made in terms of a standardised format for the cash flow statement. Each level of the statement is compared across the two samples of companies to determine whether there are significant differences. The ratios compared are those identified as indicative of how well management has handled certain areas of the firm's operating and financial activities that are critical to its cash position.

This study differs from existing studies in at least two important respects. First, this is one of a very few studies to look at cash flow differences between failed and non-failed firms. Second, and most important, this is the only major study which examines such differences when the cash flows are computed using the direct method of cash flow analysis as opposed to the usual indirect method used in the UK where the entry point for the analysis tends to take a measurement of profit and then add back depreciation (see Chapter 3).

It should be noted at the outset that the purpose of this study is purely descriptive. The intent is to document any significant differences in the cash flow profiles between bankrupt and non-bankrupt firms. No attempt is being made at this point to build a model for predicting bankruptcy or financial distress. Nonetheless, the significant differences observed in the cash flow profiles and the selected ratios of the two groups of companies suggest that the results reported below can be used as another element in the cash flow analysis process.

Review of the cash flow statement

In November 1987 the Financial Accounting Standards Board (FASB) adopted Statement of Financial Accounting Standards No. 95, 'Statement of Cash Flows,' which requires the inclusion of a statement of cash flows whenever a full set of financial statements is prepared. A similar requirement (UK FRS1) was implemented in Great Britain from March 1992. The FASB pronouncement permits one of two methods – the direct or the indirect – for calculating cash flows. Under the direct method, the actual cash inflows and outflows associated with operating activities are presented. The new accounting rules encourage this method of presentation but also permit an indirect method of calculation that starts with net income and makes a series of adjustments for depreciation, deferred taxes, gains and losses on sales of equipment and businesses, and changes in working capital.

The direct approach

A direct method for calculating cash flows, the UCA cash flow statement, is highly structured and reveals the actual cash inflow or outflow of each item on the income statement. The calculation of cash net income begins with taking cash receipts from sales and then makes deductions for payments to suppliers, employees, creditors, stockholders, and to the Government for taxes. With its focus on actual cash flows and its specific identification of such items as cash flow from sales activity, cash cost of goods sold, and mandatory debt retirement, it yields additional information on the structure of cash flows that cannot be found in an indirect approach. Also, its standardised format facilitates comparisons across firms.

CASE STUDY: GRAY MANUFACTURING

To illustrate the UCA cash flow statement and its interpretation, consider the following example of Gray Manufacturing Company, one of the firms in the sample of bankrupt companies. This firm was involved in the manufacture and sale of outdoor metal storage buildings, metal partitions, and metal refuse containers. It was also a contractor for the construction and renovation of large municipal incinerators and was active in the development of techniques to control beach erosion.

During the first six months of 1975, Gray Manufacturing experienced accrual losses of $1.8 million and began to run into cash flow problems due to start-up difficulties at the new manufacturing headquarters of one of its divisions. In October 1975, after one of its institutional lenders called the balance on a promissory note because of a covenant violation and the IRS filed a tax lien against it, Gray sought court protection under Chapter 11 of the Federal Bankruptcy Act.

Gray's balance sheets and income statements for the period 1969–1974 were used to calculate its cash flow statements and selected ratios for the period 1970–1974. The cash flow statements in the table below follow the

UCA format, and the ratios are those that the UCA text identifies as deserving of special scrutiny.

GRAY MANUFACTURING COMPANY – CASH FLOW STATEMENTS

$	1970	1971	1972	1973	1974	Cumulative
Operating flows						
Net sales	14,587	14,626	16,225	33,418	32,588	111,444
Change in accounts	−99	397	−1,619	−883	1,003	−1,201
1. Cash flow from sales	14,488	15,023	14,606	32,535	33,591	110,243
Cost of goods sold	−11,622	−11,336	−12,596	−26,703	−29,685	−91,942
Change in inventories	1,458	−167	−1,455	−5,232	−1,668	−7,064
Change in accounts payable	−18	25	617	2,034	1,437	4,095
2. Cash cost of goods	−10,182	−11,478	−13,434	−29,901	−29,916	−94,911
3. Cash gross profit	4,306	3,545	1,172	2,634	3,675	15,332
Sell., gen., & admin. expenses	−2,697	−2,649	−2,721	−5,193	−5,278	−18,538
Change in prepaid assets	56	−55	−48	−282	155	−174
Change in other accruals	7	135	76	42	−125	135
4. Cash operating expenses	−2,634	−2,569	−2,693	−5,433	−5,248	−18,577
5. Cash operating income	1,672	976	−1,521	−2,799	−1,573	−3,245
6. Misc. cash income (expense)	1,293	419	960	−73	281	2,880
Income taxes	−52	−197	−302	−321	509	−363
Change in accrued inc taxes	−310	110	276	−14	−256	−194
Change in deferred inc taxes	404	173	−79	−82	−536	−120
7. Cash income	42	86	−105	−417	−283	−677
8. Cash flow from operations	3,007	1,481	−666	−3,289	−1,575	−1,042
Financing costs						
Interest expense	−347	−385	−496	−684	−989	−2,901
Common dividends	0	−680	−51	−497	0	−1,228
9. Total financing costs	−347	−1,065	−547	−1,181	−989	−4,129
10. Thousands	2,660	416	−1,213	−4,470	−2,564	−5,171
11. Mandatory debt retirement	−200	−565	−180	−302	−372	−1,619
12. Cash flow after debt retire.	2,460	−149	−1,393	−4,772	−2,936	−6,790

Investment activity

Net capital expenditures	−142	−102	−281	−1,754	−426	−2,705
Change in long term invests.	−3,949	110	479	1,408	−589	−2,541
13. Tot. invest. activity cash flow	−4,091	8	198	−346	−1,015	−5,246
14. Cash flow before financing	−1,631	−141	−1,195	−5,118	−3,951	−12,036

Financing activity

Changes in notes payable	−18	0	300	2,162	4,183	6,627
Change in long-term debt	3,595	156	354	263	−69	4,299
Change in other liabilities	−178	0	0	1,642	−289	1,175
Change in common stock	0	285	−327	764	20	742
15. Total financing cash flow	3,399	441	327	4,831	3,845	12,843
16. Change in cash	1,768	300	−868	−287	−106	807
Beginning cash	402	2,170	2,470	1,602	1,315	402
Ending cash	2,170	2,470	1,602	1,315	1,209	1,209

This information provides a number of clues about what went wrong for Gray. With sales more than doubling between 1972 and 1973, the compound rate of sales growth over 1969–1974 was 13.5%. This growth was accompanied by a deteriorating gross margin and an apparent lack of attention to inventory control. After a drop in 1971, cost of goods sold/net sales increased to 91.1%. The average age of inventory rose steadily from 57 days in 1970 to 127 days in 1974. Despite an improvement in the collection period and a not so surprising lengthening of the age of accounts payable, Gray's cash margin fell and its cash operating income weakened as a result.

CASH FLOW ANALYSIS OF A MANUFACTURING COMPANY

Example:	1970	1971	1972	1973	1974
Cash operating income	$1672	$976	($1521)	($2799)	($1573)
Cash income taxes	$42	$86	($105)	($417)	($283)
Net cash flow from operations	$3007	$1481	($606)	($3289)	($1575)
Cash net income	$2660	($416)	($1213)	($4470)	($2564)
Cash flow after debt repayments	$2460	($149)	($1393)	($4772)	($2936)
Age of accounts payable	23 days	24 days	40 days	47 days	60 days
Cash coverage ratio	55 x	−0.9 x	−0.9 x	−2.2 x	−1.2 x

Cash operating income declined and went into the red beginning in 1972. That the significant contributing causes were mismanagement of the gross margin and a lack of inventory control is best understood by considering what would have been the case if these areas had been managed more efficiently. The maintenance of cost of goods sold/net sales at its 1970 level of 79.7% and the age of inventory at its 1970 level of 57 days would have freed up additional cash of $8.8 million, resulting in cash operating income of $5.6 million for the five year period.

Taking the effect of miscellaneous cash flows and cash income taxes into account, Gray's net cash flow from operations exhibited the same pattern as its cash operating income, and the cumulative total amounted to –$1.0 million. Its interest expense, dividends, and mandatory debt retirement were completely covered by net cash flow from operations only in 1970 when the cash coverage was 5.5 times. The cash coverage ratio dropped to 0.9 times in 1971 and reached a low of –2.2 times in 1973.

In the last three years of the five year period, Gray was clearly in the position of having to arrange external financing not only for its capital expenditures but also to meet current debt maturities, pay interest and dividends, stay current on its taxes and fund operating deficits. The bulk of the $12.0 million needed for the entire five years was raised through notes payable of $6.6 million and long-term debts payable of $4.3 million.

Analysis

The preceding discussion of Gray Manufacturing's cash flow statements and the selected ratios seems to indicate that there were signs of financial distress well before its Chapter 11 filing in October 1975. However, this statement ignores information about where Gray stood in relation to the cash flows and ratios of other firms in the industry.

The question is whether or not Gray's cash flows and selected ratios in the years prior to bankruptcy were significantly different from those of similar firms (over the same period) which remained out of bankruptcy. This question was then explored for bankrupt versus non-bankrupt firms in general.

Description of sample

A sample of 60 bankrupt industrial companies that failed over the period 1973–1985 was identified from the COMPUSTAT research file and other sources such as the Wall Street Journal Index. Bankrupt utilities, transportation companies, and financial services companies were excluded because they are structurally different.

In selecting non-bankrupt firms for a control sample, the sizes of the bankrupt and non-bankrupt samples were required to approximate the relative proportions of these two types of firm in the US economy. Since a previous study reported that the median ratio of non-bankrupt to bankrupt firms over all industries is approximately four to one, an attempt was made to match each bankrupt company with four non-bankrupt firms in the same or a similar industry. However, due to a lack of data, this was not possible. Consequently, the sample of non-bankrupt firms consists of 204 industrials.

Balance sheet and income statements data for both samples were obtained from the COMPUSTAT annual industrial files. For each bankrupt firm, the cash flow statements and selected ratios were calculated for each of the five years prior to bankruptcy. Similar computations for each non-bankrupt company in the same or a similar industry were made using financial data taken from time periods contemporaneous with the related bankrupt company.

The non-bankrupt firms in the sample are, on average, much larger than the bankrupt firms in terms of both net sales and total assets. Thus, in comparing the cash flows of the sample of bankrupt firms with those of the non-bankrupt firms, it was necessary to control for differences in cash flows due to size considerations alone. To accomplish this, each item in the UCA cash flow statement in each year was scaled by total assets. Scaling by net sales and by cash flow from sales activity were also examined, but since the results of the statistical tests are similar, only those based on scaling by total assets are reported below.

In general, the results of the cash flow comparisons are highly significant. Cash operating income, cash income taxes, and cash flow after mandatory debt retirement (each scaled by total assets) were significantly higher, on average, for the non-bankrupt sample than for the bankrupt sample in each of the five years examined. Differences in net cash flow from operations and cash net income are statistically significant in four of the five years. Moving higher on the UCA cash flow statement format tends to decrease the significance of the differences somewhat. Differences in cash gross profit are significant in only three of the five years. The variables for which no statistically significant differences appear in any of the five years are cash flow from sales activity, cash cost of goods sold, and cash operating expenses.

Two of the ratios (age of accounts payable and the cash coverage ratio) are statistically significant in each of the five years prior to bankruptcy. The differences observed in the cash margin ratio are not statistically significant in any year.

Key indicators:

- Cash operating income
- Cash income taxes
- Net cash flow from operations
- Cash net income (after finance costs and dividends)
- Cash flow after debt repayments
- Age of accounts payable
- Cash coverage ratio formula:

$$\frac{\text{net cash flow from operations}}{\text{int. expense + div. + debt repay.}}$$

Data source: 1988 Gahlon & Vigeland(US)

Fig 6.3 Warning Signs Using Cash Flow Analysis (Direct Method)

Conclusion

This study establishes that these UCA cash flow variables and suggested ratios capture statistically significant differences between bankrupt and non-bankrupt firms, on average, as much as five years prior to bankruptcy. As a result, they are strong candidates for inclusion in the early warning systems of any type of corporate cash flow analysis.

An issue of great importance is 'how does a company cope with a cash crisis?' Whether the crisis is foreseen or not, a key element in the survival plan is how to cope with this event and furthermore, how to communicate recovery procedures.

CASH CRISIS MANAGEMENT

When a crisis strikes an organisation, many outside influences hinder its ability to communicate this message. These influences include confidentiality, deadlines, stress, and human emotion. Perhaps the most important task in managing a corporate crisis is conveying a company's key messages, in a coherent, disciplined and organised fashion. The CEO who has a communications blueprint on hand has already taken a major step towards mastering the challenge of a corporate crisis. The communications matrix, or message action plan (MAP), is such a blueprint.

MESSAGE ACTION PLAN
XYZ CORPORATION

	Core Message(s)	Supporting Messages	Phone Calls	Press Interviews	Press release	Letters	Meetings	Advertising	Responsibility	Timing
Board of Directors					*		*		e.g. Chairman,	e.g. Today
Division Presidents										
Regulatory Agencies			*							
Plant Management	*	*			*					
Key customers	*		*							
Key suppliers			*							
Key Shareholders										
Industry Analysts										
Sales Reps										
National Media										
Local Media		*			*					
HQ Employees		*								
Plant/Div. Employees										
Union Officials	*									
Financial Community								*		
Other Customers										
Other Suppliers										
Other Shareholders										
Retirees										
Community	*									

The MAP can avoid this problem by combining all elements of a public relations or communications plan into a single, easily read document, allowing for a quick understanding of what must be accomplished, as well as how, when and by whom.

Elements of a MAP

A communications matrix includes target audiences, message elements, communication techniques, responsibilities, time and schedule commitments, and accountability factors. They are defined as follows:

Targets

Every group to be targeted in the public relations effort should be listed in order of importance. You can set priorities in two ways: either listing the audiences on the matrix from top to bottom, or separating the constituent groups into broad categories such as primary, secondary and marginal. The second method can short-circuit endless discussions about which public is really the most important.

Message elements

List the concepts to be communicated to target audiences next to relevant publics. The idea is to keep this to one page. A core message – a capsulisation of key concepts to be communicated to all publics – is the first step in developing this portion of the plan.

Techniques

In order to avoid overlooking any possible solutions, begin by thinking in broad categories. These include: media relations and publicity, publications and other printed materials, audio and video communications, personal contacts and paid media advertising (for public relations purposes only). List the specific tactics on the matrix.

Responsibility

Who is going to accomplish each task? Often the assignment will go to more than one person and might involve personnel from the public relations department, from other corporate departments involved with the project, or from a firm acting on your client's behalf. Clarifying who's in charge will lessen the chances of overlooking opportunities and missing deadlines.

Timing

Note how long it should take for your message to reach each audience. Other key intermediate deadlines might also be listed. If the matrix is for a project covering a relatively short period of time, then all intermediate schedule and timing commitments should be listed, too.

Evaluation/Accountability

Once the immediate crisis has passed you should determine the success of the project, campaign or programme. Surveys and other ongoing measuring devices should be listed. The matrix lays out all tasks and responsibilities and provides an easy reference for evaluating staff. You can use this information to adjust your MAP to prepare for future crises.

The result will be a more controlled and consistent programme effort. Many communications inefficiencies which seem to creep into crisis programme management will be reduced. Everyone will perform more productively, and the company will communicate more effectively with the vital audiences that affect its future.

A DIFFERENT APPROACH TO CASH FLOW ANALYSIS – CASE STUDY: TANDY

The trend of sales, working capital and net income can diverge from the trend in cash flows from operations. When it does, a corporate's appearance of success may be misleading. The prudent corporate manager will incorporate each of these measures in his or her analysis.

Tandy, parent of the Radio Shack stores, was recently ranked number four in return on equity in Fortune's list of 500 top service companies. But during 1983, the company lost almost one-half its share value in the span of a few months. (Tandy's market valuation subsequently rebounded.) At this time, overall market indexes were increasing. We can use this historical data to see if cash flow analysis would have predicted the dramatic price fall earlier than traditional financial statement analysis.

The table opposite summarises information from Tandy's annual reports from 1980 to 1982. Tandy shows nicely increasing sales, profits and working capital for each year. Financial ratios of profitability and liquidity were similarly optimistic. In 1982, net income was 11% of sales and current assets were almost four times current liabilities. What, then, could alert us to potential trouble?

FINANCIAL DATA – TANDY CORPORATION

(Millions of dollars) Balance sheet	1980	1981	1982
Current assets			
Accounts receivable and trade notes	26	42	84
Inventory	435	514	671
Total current assets	461	556	755
Current liabilities			
Accounts payable	59	55	64
Accrued expenses	59	67	92
Taxes payable	25	47	53
Total current liabilities	143	169	208
Income statement			
Sales	1392	1707	2061
Net income	112	170	224
Statement of changes in financial position			
Working capital from operations (net income + depreciation & other minor adjustments)	131	201	260

The table overleaf presents a simple cash flow worksheet, based on the financial data shown above. We see a problem. Cash flow from operations dropped by one-quarter in 1982. Further, we can see why: inventory growth used up $157 million of operating cash. This is double that of the previous years and not justified by the sales increase. The share price did not drop until months later, when management admitted to the inventory build-up. This example shows that cash flow can be an early indication of problems.

   Some commentators have challenged the importance of cash flow analysis. In a widely discussed Harvard Business Review article, two researchers reported that declining or negative cash flow, while strongly related to firms that subsequently failed, was also frequently found in successful firms. Thus, they claimed that the predictive ability of cash flow analysis was virtually nil.

CASH FLOW ANALYSIS – TANDY CORPORATION

(Millions of dollars) Balance sheet	1980	1981	1982
Sales	1396	1707	2061
Net income	112	170	224
Adjustments*	+19	+31	+36
Working capital from operations	131	201	260
Accounts receivable	−11	−16	−42
Inventory	−53	−4	+9
Accounts payable	+25	−4	+9
Accruals	+7	+8	+25
Taxes payable	+11	+22	+5
Cash flow from operations	110	132	100

* Add depreciation, losses on asset sales. Subtract gains on asset sales.

Numerous letters to the editor pointed out that any technique good at predicting failure certainly has merit. More important, good analysis does not focus on a single number. For example, firms in a seasonal business or those that are growing rapidly can show low cash flows for a time. However, declining cash flows without compensating increases in accounting profitability can precede trouble.

Cash flow from operations can be reconciled to the balance sheet change in cash by adding or subtracting cash flows from investing activities and from financing activities. Changes in all non-operating balance sheet items should be examined to determine the investing and financing cash flows.

Reconciling cash flow from operations to the actual change in cash has two important uses. First, the investing and financing activities of the firm give the lender valuable insights into management's activities and strategy. Second, if you can reconcile cash flow from operations to the net change in cash, you can be confident that cash flow from operations was computed correctly.

Cash flow from operations should be used in concert with sales and net income trends to evaluate past performance and to project needs in the future. Cash flows should not be used in isolation. In the Harvard Business Review article mentioned above, the researchers looked at cash flow only. They found that low or negative cash flow for up to five years before bankruptcy did little by itself to distinguish firms that fail from those that survive.

Of course this is true. Successful firms that are growing rapidly can have negative cash flows when increasing receivables and inventories consume cash. Cyclical and seasonal firms can experience low cash flows when their sales are the best. Cash flow patterns are meaningful only when compared to sales and actual profitability trends. Rising sales with constant profit margins can justify falling cash flows. Constant or falling sales combined with low or negative cash flows are unacceptable. The constant financing of negative cash flows must eventually lead to failure.

CASH FLOW AND THE TURNAROUND CONSULTANT

At the Frank Hawkins Kenan Institute of Private Enterprise at the University of North Carolina an unusual 18 month study of sick companies took place, looking at what consultants can do to diagnose their ills and suggest cures. A business in decline needs competent professional advice from an impartial consultant who is familiar with the entire turnaround process.

The study team interviewed more than 80 nationally known turnaround managers, reviewed some 600 articles, and analysed 300 case studies. This narrative summarises the findings.

The epidemic of business troubles produced some startling data. Chapter 11 bankruptcy filings jumped from 16,622 in 1982 to 21,370 in 1986. During the same period, Chapter 7 filings rose from 257,644 to 374,452. This all occurred in an expanding economy and during a business-friendly administration.

The paramount problem is not seeing trouble ahead before it becomes intractable.

Business failure begins with early signals of decline which are often unobserved or ignored. Many businesses which are in decline are not aware of it because their management has not noticed either the internal or external signals of decline. Research confirms the requirement that, especially in near-turnaround circumstances, it is critical to pay attention to those internal and external elements affecting the success of a business.

Internal elements – including the basic business functions – are most easily controlled by management, though, paradoxically, often poorly controlled. External elements – considered to be uncontrollable – include legal, political, cultural, social, competitive, economic, geographical, and technological factors. Each of these can influence a business and each sends distinct signals of prospective change which may signal decline for a business.

Some businesses survive the changes while others fail. The difference is attributable to planning based on understanding the particular signals of decline.

Watch for early warning signals

Both the internal and external elements exhibit early warning signals which predict business decline. The most common warning signals that the turn-around consultant uses to analyse the extent of external elements are:

- measures of economic growth, which give management an indication as to economic climate influencing expansion plans;
- credit availability and money market activity, which indicate trends in commercial and investment banking in relation to the financial needs of a business;
- capital market activity, giving a clear signal to management of the attitude of investors toward a given industry, and which signals the investment community's belief regarding the business climate;
- business demographics, which can alert management to the numbers of businesses entering and leaving a given industry, and which can be used as an indicator of the expansion or contraction of the market and competitive size of the industry;
- price level changes; indicating the rate of inflation, which influences consumption and therefore can have an impact on production;
- changes in the competitive structure of the marketplace, affecting products, pricing, marketing, and distribution;
- changing technology, whereby rapid breakthroughs and changes in products, production, marketing, and distribution are possible;
- cultural and social changes, which can alter consumer preferences or conditions under which a product can be sold;
- legal and political changes, such that a market can be adversely affected, thereby impacting on production, sale, or distribution of a product.

The turnaround consultant who recognises such external signals must be able to draft a turnaround plan which addresses their consequences. The planning process is more than plotting a course around the external elements; it is a course charted for profitability despite the new obstacles. Many businesses have strategic plans that become useless because they are not adaptable to changing external conditions.

The internal elements of finance, management, marketing, and distribution may be, or may just seem to be, easier to examine. Finance, production, marketing, and distribution are those elements most frequently used as levers by turnaround consultants. Management is the force that drives these functions, and yet management is often at the root of business failures.

The internal elements are dynamic, and yet research indicates that when decline occurs there is a lack of control over them. Decline does not happen overnight; rather it occurs in stages.

The early decline stage is the first indication of trouble. Profits are decreasing but management does not analyse the possible causes. The profit decrease is perceived as a temporary phenomenon which will be self-correcting. Reductions continue until profits disappear. In mid-term decline, losses increase and management becomes concerned. Causes for decline are discussed and some actions may be taken. In the event that action is not taken, the business slides into late decline. Here, losses erode capital reserves, cash flow is negative and management is scurrying to prevent collapse of the business.

Early decline is signalled by the following developments, typically by several at a time:

- shortage of cash for meeting current obligations;
- current assets decreasing concurrent with current liabilities increasing, reducing working capital;
- increase in accounts payable aging;
- increase in accounts receivable aging;
- return on investment decreasing by 20–30%;
- lack of sales growth;
- several quarters of losses;
- quarters of losses exceeding those of profits (either in dollars or number) over the preceding year or two;
- increase in employee absenteeism and accidents;
- increase in customer complaints regarding product quality, delivery, back-orders, running out of stock, or service;
- late financial and management information.

Mid-term decline is signalled by these developments:

- inventory increasing and sales decreasing;
- financial margins eroding, as revenue decreases and expenses continue to increase;
- advances from banks increasing in dollar amount and frequency;
- financial and management information unreliable, as well as late;
- customer confidence declining and the customer base noticeably eroding;

- vendors demanding payment on delinquent accounts and placing the business on a cash basis;
- bank overdrafts become a form of interim financing;
- paying accounts delayed by opportunistic customers;
- loan covenants violated and compliance with all loan covenants demanded by banks;
- bank borrowing more frequently used to cover payroll;
- interest rates on indebtedness increased by banks, owing to increased risk.

By the time of late decline, the following will be occurring:

- profit decreases ignored by management and attempts to raise cash made;
- attempts made to reduce operating costs, without analysing the causes of business problems;
- overdrawn bank accounts becoming permanent loans;
- cash crisis;
- accounts payable 60 to 90 days late;
- accounts receivable 90+ days late;
- further decline in sales owing to loss of customer confidence;
- employee morale extremely low;
- company credibility eroded;
- inventory turnover excessive, with inventory supply down;
- suppliers requiring payment prior to delivery;
- fewer reports issued to the bank;
- auditors qualifying their opinion of latter;
- cheques returned because of insufficient funds;
- further decrease in financial margins, indicating imminent bankruptcy;
- further cash flow negatives;
- increase in uncollectable receivables as customers find new suppliers;
- management team trying to convince lenders that company is viable and that liquidation or bankruptcy is not called for.

The inevitable result of management's inability to recognise and confront decline is, of course, deterioration of the business. As stakeholders become more aware of the business's inability to maintain its ongoing operations and finances, they become reticent and eventually unwilling to be associated with it. This loss of credibility in the business community can be, and typically is, devastating. While decline continues, chaos takes the place of management reasoning and planning, leaving few options for the major stakeholders to pursue. Bankruptcy is a possible alternative. More frequently, however, in today's business environment, a turnaround consultant is called in. The initiative and initial contact can be by shareholders, a bank, a major creditor, the board of directors, or by management itself.

The turnaround consultant is willing and able to bring order out of chaos and not only save the business from further decline but return it to profitability. To accomplish this, the turnaround consultant must be able to restore credibility in the shortest possible time, relying, at least initially, upon a sound turnaround plan plus outstanding credentials. To have a fair chance for success, stakeholders must be convinced that the turnaround plan is viable and can be implemented.

The US national survey reveals that fewer than 20% of business failures were caused by external elements. The other 80% are caused by the failure of management to control the internal elements.

Management issues

Management often does not use or know how to use the managerial tools at its disposal. Consequently, the turnaround consultant must be able to build a team to manage the business, not only through its decline and return to profitability, but also after the consultant leaves, presumably through a period of business growth.

The successful turnaround team consists of people to work with every part of the business. Among other things, they need to ensure the dismissal of non-productive employees, and to ascertain where stock may be obsolete, some receivables (debtors) not collectable, assets incorrectly valued, and warranty reserves unrealistic. The stakeholders must be provided with an accurate description of the business. Once accuracy is established, then reconstruction can commence.

Not all of the symptoms noted above need to appear to signal a decline; it is sufficient cause to worry if only some of them occur. Many signals can result from the growth that a company may have experienced. Too frequently, when the growth ends and the business enters a period of stability or decline, management operates as if growth will shortly resume. When this growth fails to materialise, a gap occurs between plans and reality.

CASE STUDY: CRAZY EDDIE'S

Crazy Eddie's, a group retailing domestic appliances, was an example of a company that had both internal and external problems. Internally, there were excessive layers of management, high wages, corporate waste, cost over-runs, employee morale problems, and information flow deficiencies. In short, the company exhibited almost every internal sign of decline. Externally, new competition entered the market. There was also a slump in Crazy Eddie's markets, so revenues decreased. Since Crazy Eddie's had damaged its relationships with appliance suppliers, it was unable to obtain the merchandise necessary to compete. Recently, the company has undergone a turnaround. Part of the strategy was to cut costs and payroll by a minimum of $235 million. Internal factors were addressed by laying off unneeded managers, reducing wages, adding a profit sharing plan, settling various lawsuits on corporate waste, reducing costs, and adding a computer system to prevent the selling of items below cost. Externalities included rebuilding relationships with suppliers and banks and restoring Crazy Eddie's image in the mind of the consumer.

One part of a reorganisation involves the flow of information and analysis of the customer. Products and markets are analysed to determine relative profitability: those generating losses should be terminated. Saving position in the market is essential. A turnaround will be short-lived if the market is no longer available when restructuring is completed. Too often, people think of a turnaround as only reducing inventory, eliminating excess employees, delaying payables, collecting receivables, selling excess assets, cutting costs, and in effect merely generating cash. These procedures are worthless, however, if they destroy the business's market position.

During turnaround, a firm's most basic methods of doing business are changed. Turnaround is a hands-on process, with the turnaround consultant steering all of the functions. Research indicates that in successful turn-arounds revised budgets are created from the bottom up and accountability is strictly enforced. Actual costs are used in place of standard costing, and product contribution margins are used to determine those products which contribute the most to the fixed costs of the business. Analyses of cash flow are used continually to aid in developing (and revising) an operating plan for the business. The time frame generated and the amount of cash inflow will determine the means, and the likelihood, of the business surviving.

Reviewing accounts receivable is a critical cash flow task of the turn-around consultant. Classification of customers and aging of accounts receivable will indicate which customers are profitable. The business may have many customers it cannot afford to carry any longer; these are the ones who are continually delinquent in paying their accounts. The business may also have customers who pay on a timely basis but provide little business. These should be analysed to determine whether they should be pursued for additional orders.

Banks, vendors, customers, employees, boards of directors, and others affected by the decline of a business need to be made part of the solution. Research shows that by the time they notice that a problem exists, the situation typically is approaching crisis proportions.

Banks and boards tend to be balance sheet and income statement driven, and a healthy appearing balance sheet and income statement can disguise many problems. Banks and boards rarely visit the business and review operations, walk through the plant floor, and talk with employees. In general, they do not investigate basic financial data such as accounts receivable and payable. They tend to learn about employee morale, customer service, equipment condition, and other on-site conditions mainly from management.

Trade creditors are the business's lifeline to its supplies. When payments to them are delinquent, the business is in jeopardy. Management will argue that other suppliers can be obtained, but unless and until the underlying problem causing the delinquent payments is addressed, the reservoir of suppliers will evaporate, along with the company's credit. New suppliers require credit references, and changing suppliers bears a substantial switching cost. The new supplier has to produce or acquire the supplies requested, schedule delivery, and obtain payment. As the business adds new suppliers, the bank will receive credit report requests and may interpret this as a signal of decline.

Employee participation is essential in the turnaround process, whether management personnel or factory workers. Their work life and private life can be affected by the turnaround process. During turnaround, it may be essential to ask for pay concessions, for example. Hours of work and working conditions can be at stake. When employees participate in planning (or are at least consulted) as to how a business is to be restructured, they more readily tend to accept painful concessions. After restructuring, a business certainly is indebted to these people, and they should be recompensed.

In 1983, thirteen employees of International Harvester bought SRC. They developed a daily detailed reporting system and a full-blown cash flow statement. In 1986, sales at SRC reached $42 million. Net operating income increased to 11% and the debt to equity ratio was reduced from 89:1 to 51:1. The appraised value of a share in the company's stock ownership plan increased from $0.10 to $8.50. Absenteeism and recordable accidents almost disappeared.

When dealing with employee morale and concessions where there is a union presence, it is usually necessary to gain its cooperation. A turnaround can be accomplished without union cooperation, but sometimes not without such drastic steps as bankruptcy or massive layoffs. Union leaders are perfectly capable of understanding that cooperation is in the best interest of all parties. Their concern is for the well-being of their members and continuation of the union. Concessions regarding pay rates, hours, working conditions, raises, vacations, accumulated sick leave, or benefits will be agreed to only when union leadership and membership are convinced that the company actually can survive. Cooperation of other stakeholders with the turnaround consultant places additional pressure on the union to cooperate.

The study showed that a business in decline tends to forsake customer service. Deliveries may be late, product quality can deteriorate and back orders may be delayed. It is essential, therefore, that a turnaround consultant investigates customer satisfaction – probably through interviews or other contact with selected customers – and determines the extent to which improving customer satisfaction will play a part in the turnaround.

This is particularly important when a repricing strategy is necessary – as is often the case. Pricing affects the cash flow of the business and, accordingly, the success of the turnaround. When customer service and quality are high, customer satisfaction tends also to be high. With satisfaction and loyalty maintained or re-established through service and quality it will be possible to increase prices and have customers more readily accept these increases.

Though often overlooked by management, numerous financial ratios have a high predictive power for the turnaround consultant. The most commonly used financial ratios are:

- Working capital to total assets,
- Retained earnings to total assets,
- EBIT (earning before interest and taxes) to total assets,
- Market value of equity to book value of debt,
- Sales to total assets.

These ratios are especially useful when applied over a time period of at least three years, allowing for the establishment of patterns from which deviations can readily be discerned. A deviation serves as a red flag highlighting problems.

In reviewing the prior three years' performance, a trend analysis of the ratios can be useful. This process allows the turnaround consultant to maintain an ongoing analysis of financial trends. Once established, the procedure should be adopted by operating management. The ratios used by turnaround managers are designed to indicate the ability of the business to survive and will be of interest to investors and lenders.

A turnaround can be defined as a sustained positive change in the performance of a business to obtain a desired result; it is also the process by which a business with inadequate performance is analysed and changed to a desired result. A successful turnaround prior to a crisis avoids any form of crisis management, which is the extreme case, resulting generally in removal of top management and restructuring of financial, operational, and strategic aspects of the business.

In a turnaround, analysis and action are almost simultaneous for the consultant. The immediate requirement is to find the major problems, analyse them, and implement solutions. To help accomplish this the turnaround consultant relies on the management remaining after whatever initial purge of incompetent managers has occurred. Both groups are identified during initial analysis of a company, which may take anywhere from three days to four weeks, depending upon the size of the company and the extent of its problems.

The turnaround consultant usually works with the CEO, provided that the CEO can become part of a permanent solution. A CEO unable to assist in resolving the problems must be replaced and, in that event, the replacement is the turnaround consultant. Afterwards, a permanent CEO can be sought.

The new CEO should be made part of the turnaround team as quickly as possible, providing the turnaround consultant with the opportunity to educate the CEO regarding the causes of the business's difficulties and the implementation of the turnaround plan. The other, remaining, management personnel round out the turnaround team. Utilising existing management and focussing their energies and talents is less expensive than bringing in a crisis or turnaround team or hiring entirely new management. Furthermore, salvaging existing management leaves an experienced, competent team in place to manage the business when the turnaround is over and it is time for the turnaround consultant to leave.

Important as it is, profitability is not really the primary mission of a business; survival is. Once survival is assured, a business's mission is to create something of value that is desired in the market-place: it is creation of value that generates profits. Thus, preservation of the market during turnaround is essential.

Research has shown that the turnaround process can be driven by forces at both the strategic and the operational level. It is a vital part of the consultant's job to match the turnaround methodology to the specific situation, usually mounting the turnaround on several fronts.

A strategic turnaround will be required where forces require the redefinition of a business. Such forces could be changing markets, technological innovations, or social and political factors.

An operational turnaround usually focusses on internal characteristics of the business and aims to make improvements through such things as cost cutting, new revenue generation, or by reducing assets.

Black and Decker was involved in an operationally oriented turnaround. The company had over 100 different motor sizes. Consumer and professional tools had been split into two separate groups that seldom communicated with one another. This made it easier for the competition to establish niches where Black and Decker did not have market coverage. To remedy the situation, the company organised its plants around motor sizes. It reduced product variations and streamlined manufacturing. The number of plants were reduced from 25 to 19. Capacity utilisation increased by 75 per cent.

A financial turnaround is targeted at restructuring the financial structure or management of a business. The object is to more fully utilise inherent financial strength. ITT is an example of a financial turnaround. It divested itself of 23 businesses, realising almost $1.5 billion and an increased return on equity from eight per cent in 1979 to twelve per cent in 1987. It also slashed expenses, cutting its work force by two-thirds between 1984 and 1987. In 1987, ITT had $17.4 billion revenue.

For a turnaround consultant to be effective he must have the confidence of the board of directors and the CEO (if a privately owned corporation, a majority of shareholders) and the authority to act. As progress is made, the turnaround consultant will gradually gain the confidence of senior management, employees and other stakeholders. The ability to act without being encumbered by committees and boards helps the consultant to return the business to profitability.

Turnaround strategies identified in the study include the following:

- Revenue generating. Sales and advertising are increased, market share expanded and prices decreased.
- Product and market refocussing. Products and markets are analysed to determine their profitability; markets are analysed to determine their growth. Customers are analysed to determine the nature of purchases, payment history and ability to purchase more. Channels of distribution are analysed to determine their effectiveness. Products are analysed to determine their saleability, contribution margins, actual costs of production, cost of sale, cost of distribution, manufacturing efficiency, inventory carrying cost, and cost of customer service.

- Cost cutting. Administrative costs, R&D expenditures, and marketing costs are cut.
- Asset reduction. Unnecessary assets are removed. Usually these assets look nice on the balance sheet but actually produce maintenance costs out of line with revenue.
- Combinations of any of the above.

Knowing which approach to use and when to use it largely determines turnaround success. It may be that, initially, cost cutting is required, superseded by additional revenue generation. An inappropriate approach can be a terminal error. Some rough rules of thumb generated from the study seem to apply to most turnaround situations:

- Mature businesses should use retrenchment and efficiency strategies, not product or marketing refocussing.
- Businesses with low capacity utilisation should pursue cost cutting strategies.
- Businesses with high capacity utilisation should pursue revenue enhancement as well as cost cutting strategies.
- Businesses with high market share should pursue revenue generating strategies and product or market refocussing.

In the short run, a turnaround plan can and should supersede a business's long-range strategic plan. However, once a turnaround is complete, the strategic planning process should be reinstated. Creation of a 'living' strategic plan is essential to ongoing success of the business.

Not all turnaround consultants agree on the time that should be allotted to implementing a turnaround plan, but in general there are five stages in a turnaround:

- evaluation of the situation
- creating a plan
- implementation of the plan
- stabilisation of the business
- return to growth of the business

Often the turnaround manager has to be an autocrat, one whose instincts and skills guide the business through its difficulties. Though autocracy could have been part of the problem, the turnaround manager's autocracy is necessary, albeit temporary, to be able to deal with the key issues.

The ability to deal with many problems and people simultaneously and under pressure is a skill developed by the turnaround consultant over a long period of time. Rapidly developing an understanding of the abilities of the employees and being able to mould them into a team is essential. Knowing how to negotiate with bankers, lawyers, vendors, and other stakeholders is one of the key elements of success.

It must be remembered that the normal employment of a turnaround consultant is to deal only with failing business and with crisis situations. The rendering of general business advice and consulting assistance is left to other management consulting specialists. In examining survival in cash crisis situations therefore.

Choosing a turnaround consultant is not easy, although there are many who are prepared to take on turnaround assignments.

CASH FLOW AND REFINANCING – CASE STUDY: LAURA ASHLEY

Laura Ashley is one of the few genuinely international retail groups head-quartered in the UK. At the end of its last financial year, it had a total of 481 outlets worldwide, with more shops in North America than in the UK, a significant continental European presence and a successful Japanese joint-venture operating 24 (now 35) shops. Its principal business is the design, manufacture and sale of garments, home furnishings and fragrances. Total revenue last year was £296.6 million.

Laura Ashley's difficulties in the early part of 1990 had been well publicised. Suffice it to say that, by the middle of the year, its financial position was becoming serious. Borrowings had risen to approximately 122% of shareholders' funds and the group had undergone a difficult renegotiation of its bank facilities, leaving it with a highly restrictive and short-term borrowing structure. There was also an urgent requirement to return the business to its core activities and to rationalise its cost base, both of which would be hard to achieve within the confines of its revised loan facilities.

As a result, the Laura Ashley management had concluded by mid-1990 that additional capital was required to achieve the reorganisation and to see the group through the current retail downturn.

In total, an estimated £40 million–£50 million of new equity capital was required compared with a stock market valuation for the whole group at that time of approximately £100 million. The Ashley family and related trusts held approximately 70% of the equity, which meant that the shares had little liquidity and an artificially low price. The usual sources of new equity capital were not readily available.

A rights issue to existing shareholders was not practicable, both because of the amount required in relation to the market capitalisation – particularly if the Ashley family were not to take up their rights – and the consequently severe dilution for shareholders who did not subscribe. It would also have been extremely difficult to underwrite; an essential under-pinning for an issue of this nature.

A placing with a selected number of institutions or trade investors could not have been achieved on sufficiently attractive terms to justify a waiver of existing shareholders' pre-emption rights, and would almost certainly have resulted in the Ashley family's shareholding being diluted below the control level of 50%.

Disposals of peripheral businesses were likely to result in too little cash to be effective.

These difficulties were compounded by the ownership of Revman Industries, which the group bought in early 1989. Led by a talented management team, Revmans designs and manufactures fashion bedroom furnishings for sale to major department stores and other US retail outlets.

Although initially quite small in size, Revman was expanding rapidly and the need to finance its working capital requirements became a major difficulty, at one stage threatening to breach Laura Ashley's US credit facility. Laura Ashley's dilemma was that it needed to support the profit potential of Revman and its management team, but had insufficient financial resources to do so.

Faced with these financial requirements, Laura Ashley reviewed its alternatives with Dillon Read and decided that its best option was to identify a partner fulfilling the following criteria:

- It must understand the value of the Laura Ashley brand and contribute commercially as well as financially to the group;
- It must be willing and able to invest the amount of equity required;
- It must accept that the capital injection would be structured to enable the Ashley family to remain in control.

For the previous twelve months, the Aeon Group, Laura Ashley's joint-venture partner, had been watching developments in the group with increasing concern. The Aeon Group, which has a Tokyo stock market capitalisation of £2 billion, is a major Japanese stores group involved in supermarkets, speciality stores, restaurants and mail order businesses.

Interestingly, its chairman, Takuya Okada, at 65 years old is the same age as Laura Ashley's Chairman Sir Bernard Ashley and, like him, had created a major international retail group; in his case from a relatively humble family kimono business on the outskirts of Nagoya. He is also a considerable Anglophile, and was appointed a CBE in 1989 for his contribution to trade between the UK and Japan.

In view of this success, the Aeon Group was keen to develop the Laura Ashley brand further in Japan and other parts of Asia. They had been frustrated, however, by the joint-venture's limited financial resources and Laura Ashley's preoccupation with problems at home. Additionally, the Aeon Group was concerned that these difficulties might adversely affect the Japanese joint-venture or the Ashley family's ownership.

In early 1990, Dillon Read's Tokyo office approached the Aeon Group, which offered to help in whatever way Laura Ashley thought appropriate. Laura Ashley's initial response was to ask the Japanese whether they would be interested in investing in Revman. The Aeon Group agreed to this in principle and both parties appointed Dillon Read in New York to produce a valuation of the Revman business by mid-June.

The Aeon Group was, however, reluctant to make a minority investment in a Laura Ashley subsidiary without taking a larger stake in the Japanese joint-venture and participating in the capital of the quoted UK company.

After further discussions with Sir Bernard Ashley, it was agreed that the best way of reaching a sensible resolution of both parties' objectives was to arrange a private meeting in New York between the two chairmen over the weekend of 4/5 August. During the course of these discussions, a tripartite transaction was negotiated and subsequently recorded in a Heads of Agreement signed in Tokyo on 17 August 1990. The essence of this was:

– Subscription in Laura Ashley
The Aeon Group would subscribe in cash for new shares in Laura Ashley at a price of 85p per share, compared with the then market price of 49p, amounting to 15% of the issued share capital and providing Laura Ashley with total proceeds of £29 million (net of expenses)
– Right of first refusal
The Ashley family and related trusts would grant the Aeon Group a right of first refusal for one year to purchase up to five per cent of the Laura Ashley equity at a price to be negotiated at the time.
– Standstill and other protections
The Aeon Group would agree not to buy or sell any shares in Laura Ashley or make an offer for the company without the approval of the Laura Ashley board for a period of ten years, except in the case of a third party bid.

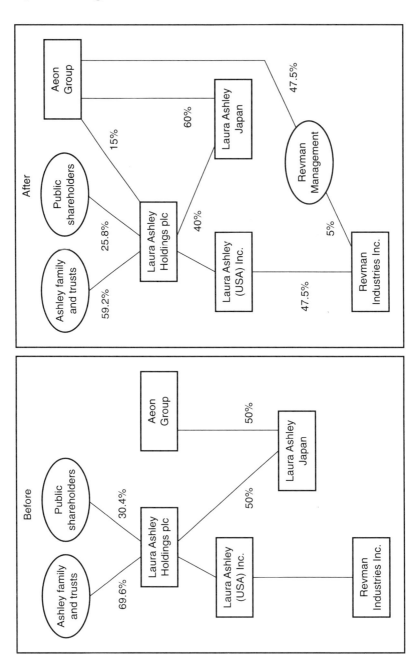

Fig 6.4 Laura Ashley Ownership Structure: Before and After

In return, the Aeon Group would be entitled to appoint one non-executive director to the Laura Ashley board and would have the right to maintain its percentage holding in any subsequent issue of new shares by the company.
– Subscription in Revman
The Aeon Group and Revman's senior management would invest approximately £9.4 million for new shares in Revman, giving them respectively 47.5% and five per cent of the equity. Laura Ashley would retain a 47.5% interest in Revman which would become an associated company, and would continue to receive royalties from sales of Laura Ashley branded goods.
– Refinancing of Revman borrowings
Revman would obtain non-recourse borrowings for approximately £17.9 million, which would be used partly to repay borrowings from Laura Ashley of approximately £14.8 million and partly to fund working capital. Laura Ashley would also be repaid £4.3 million in cash from Revman and would receive a further £4.1 million of redeemable, preference stock.
– Extension of Japanese joint-venture
The Aeon Group would purchase from Laura Ashley ten per cent of their existing Japanese joint-venture, Laura Ashley Japan, for £0.6 million in cash, thus increasing its shareholding to 60%. The scope of Laura Ashley Japan would also be extended to cover the whole of Asia and to include all of Laura Ashley's branded products. In return, the royalty rate to Laura Ashley would be increased.

The immediate financial effect of the transactions, which were completed at the end of November, has been to reduce Laura Ashley's borrowings significantly, with an associated saving in annual interest costs. On a pro forma basis, net borrowings as at 27 January 1990, dropped by 50 million and gearing reduced from 122% to 34%.

The capital investment has also enabled Laura Ashley to substitute a credit facility more suited to a public UK company, with considerably more flexibility in terms of covenants, and other restrictions than the straitjacket imposed in the middle of the year. Confident that the new facility would be put in place, the management were able to embark on a significant cost reduction exercise in September.

In the Aeon Group, Laura Ashley has obtained a partner who understands the quality of the Laura Ashley brand and, with its Far Eastern presence and size, has the local retailing experience and financial resources to expand Laura Ashley Japan in a potentially major new market for its products. Laura Ashley will be able to benefit from these developments not only through its 40% stake in the joint-venture but also through increased royalty income.

Finally, the Ashley family has maintained its close identification with the company and workforce by retaining control. After the subscription by the Aeon Group, their shareholding reduces to approximately 59% of the equity and, on exercise of the right of first refusal, falls to approximately 54%. Equally, the Aeon Group with 15% of the equity (potentially rising to 20%) and a non-executive director on the Board has an influential stake.

It is a delicate balance but one which provides the company and the Ashley family with maximum flexibility, while ensuring that the Aeon Group is able to share in the future of this British company.

In this chapter readers will have seen there is much to be gained by studying cash flow management techniques from the USA. In particular we have looked at:

- The Du-Pont pyramid of ratios;
- Monitoring cash flow ratios using a computerised spreadsheet (case study JN Nichols – Vimto);
- Corporate cash generation abilities and the fallback margin of safety in terms of cash flow;
- The levels of sales growth that a corporate can sustain from internally generated cash flow – using the sustainable growth ratio;
- Early warning signals using cash flow analysis;
- Key cash flow ratios;
- Cash crisis management using a Message Action Plan;

and finally

- Cash flow and the turnaround consultant.

CONCLUSION

As you will have seen from this book CASH IS KING and therefore the strategic management of cash flow is essential to the survival of any business be it large or small.

Within this book we have looked at the place of cash flow within a business, examining the elements of the cash flow cycle and the consequences of high gearing levels, and the effects of competitive strategy and industry competition on cash flow – reviewing the case study Hi-Tec Sports incorporating the new FRS1 cash flow statement.

We then looked at ways of squeezing more cash from operational cash flow and working investment and business cycles; a review was made of capital expenditure methods of appraisal and how to monitor liquidity with particular emphasis on debtors, creditors and stock. A business with liquidity out of control was analysed together with cash receipts on break-up.

We then moved into the uncertain areas of future cash flow forecasting. Two project case studies incorporating cash flow forecasts were analysed and sensitised; we then discussed longer term cash flow planning and economic life-cycles using the cash tank method and computerised spreadsheets.

Crisis in terms of cash flow was the next area to be studied: we reviewed predicting corporate failure models and followed this with cash flow issues in the development and diversification of the corporate using the Ansoff's matrix in conjunction with the Nor Western Group case study. The BCG matrix was used to pinpoint the different business units within the Nor Western case study and the case study concluded with an investigating accountant's report.

In the final section of the book we looked at cash flow lessons that can be learnt from the USA, and we examined Du-Pont analysis, cash generation and the margin of safety in terms of fall-back in cash flow. Predicting the level of sustainable sales growth was considered together with early warning signals using cash flow analysis and cash flow ratios. Cash crisis management and using Message Action Plans followed on from this, and finally we looked at cash flow and the turnaround consultant providing re-financing ideas.

Remember that cash is the essential fuel to drive the business – without it the business will certainly fail.

Remember that cash does not flow of its own accord – it can only do so as a direct consequence of management decisions . . . taken either consciously and positively or unconsciously by default.

I hope this book has proved useful to you – good luck and every success with your cash management!

APPENDIX I: FRS1 – CASH FLOW STATEMENTS

OBJECTIVE

The objective of the FRS is to require reporting entities falling within its scope to report on a standard basis their cash generation and cash absorption for any period. To this end reporting entities are required to provide a primary financial statement analysing cash flows under the standard headings of 'operating activities', 'returns on investments and servicing of finance', 'taxation', 'investing activities' and 'financing', disclosed in that sequence, in order to assist users of the financial statements in their assessment of the reporting entity's liquidity, viability and financial adaptability. The objective of the standard headings is to ensure that cash flows are reported in a form that highlights the significant components of cash flow and facilitates comparison of the cash flow performance of different businesses.

DEFINITIONS

Cash

Cash in hand and deposits repayable on demand with any bank or other financial institution. Cash includes cash in hand and deposits denominated in foreign currencies.

Cash equivalents

Short-term highly liquid investments which are readily convertible into known amounts of cash without notice and which were within three months of maturity when acquired; less advances from banks repayable within three months from the date of the advance. Cash equivalents include investments and advances denominated in foreign currencies provided that they fulfil the above criteria.

Cash flow

An increase or decrease in an amount of cash or cash equivalent resulting from a transaction.

STATEMENT OF STANDARD ACCOUNTING PRACTICE

Reporting entities falling within the scope of the paragraph below are required to provide as a primary statement within the reporting entity's financial statements a cash flow statement drawn up in accordance with the standard accounting principles set out below.

SCOPE

This FRS applies to all financial statements intended to give a true and fair view of the financial position and profit or loss (or income and expenditure) except those of entities that are:

(a) companies incorporated under the Companies Acts and entitled to the exemptions available in Sections 246 to 249 of the Companies Act 1985 for small companies when filing accounts with the Registrar of Companies, or

(b) entities which would have come under category (a) above had they been companies incorporated under companies legislation, or

(c) wholly owned subsidiary undertakings of a parent undertaking which is established under the law of a member State of the European Community where

(i) the parent undertaking publishes, in English, consolidated financial statements which include the subsidiary undertaking concerned, drawn up in accordance with United Kingdom or Republic of Ireland companies legislation or the EC Seventh Company Law Directive, and

(ii) those consolidated financial statements include a consolidated cash flow statement dealing with the cash flows of the group, and

(iii) that cash flow statement gives sufficient information to enable a user of the financial statements to derive the totals of the amounts required to be shown under each of the standard headings set out in this FRS, or

(d) Building Societies, as defined by the Building Societies Act 1986 in the United Kingdom and by the Building Societies Act 1989 in the Republic of Ireland, but only so long as they are required by law to prepare as part of their financial statements a statement of source and application of funds in a prescribed format, or

(e) mutual life assurance companies.

The cash flow statement provided with group financial statements should reflect the cash flows of the group.

Insurance companies, other than mutual life assurance companies to which the FRS does not apply, should include the cash flows of their long-term life, pensions and annuity business only to the extent that the cash flows are those of the insurance company itself rather than cash flows of the long-term funds.

PREPARATION OF CASH FLOW STATEMENTS

The cash flow statement should include all the reporting entity's inflows and outflows of cash and cash equivalents except those movements within cash and cash equivalents that result from the purchase and sale for cash or cash equivalents of holdings which form part of that entity's cash equivalents. Transactions which do not result in cash flows of the reporting entity should not be reported in the cash flow statement.

FORMAT FOR CASH FLOW STATEMENTS

The cash flow statement should list the inflows and outflows of cash and cash equivalents for the period classified under the following standard headings:

operating activities
returns on investments and servicing of finance
taxation
investing activities, and
financing

in that order and showing a total for each standard heading and a total of the net cash inflow or outflow before financing. Examples of formats for cash flow statements are provided in the illustrative examples annexed to the FRS.

CLASSIFICATION OF CASH FLOWS

The cash flow statement should disclose separately, where material, the individual categories of cash flows under the standard headings set out below except in the extremely rare circumstances where this presentation would not be a fair representation of the activities of the reporting entity. In such cases informed judgement should be used to devise an appropriate alternative treatment. The cash flow classifications may be subdivided further to give a fuller description of the activities of the reporting entity or to provide segmental information.

Where a cash flow is not specified in the categories set out below then it should be shown under the most appropriate standard heading.

CLASSIFICATION OF CASH FLOWS BY STANDARD HEADING

(i)   Operating activities

Cash flows from operating activities are in general the cash effects of transactions and other events relating to operating or trading activities. Net cash flow from operating activities represents the net increase or decrease in cash and cash equivalents resulting from the operations shown in the profit and loss account in arriving at operating profit.

Operating cash flows may be reported in the cash flow statement on a net or gross basis.

A reconciliation between the operating profit (for non-financial companies normally profit before interest) reported in the profit and loss account and the net cash flow from operating activities should be given as a note to the cash flow statement. This reconciliation should disclose separately the movements in stocks, debtors and creditors related to operating activities and other differences between cash flows and profits.

(ii) Returns on investments and servicing of finance

'Returns on investments and servicing of finance' are receipts resulting from the ownership of an investment and payments to providers of finance excluding those items required to be classified under operating, investing or financing activities.

Cash inflows from returns on investments and servicing of finance include:

(a) interest received, including any related tax recovered
(b) dividends received (disclosing separately dividends received from equity accounted entities), net of any tax credits.

Cash outflows from returns on investments and servicing of finance include:

(a) interest paid (whether or not the charge is capitalised), including any tax deducted and paid to the relevant tax authority
(b) dividends paid, excluding any advance corporation tax
(c) the interest element of finance lease rental payments.

(iii) Taxation

The cash flows included under the heading taxation are cash flows to or from taxation authorities in respect of the reporting entity's revenue and capital profits. Cash flows in respect of other taxation, including payments and receipts in respect of Value Added Tax, other sales taxes, property taxes and other taxes not assessed on the profits of the reporting entity, should be dealt with as set out in separate paragraphs of the FRS.

Taxation cash inflows include cash receipts from the relevant tax authority of tax rebates, claims or returns of overpayments.

Taxation cash outflows include cash payments to the relevant tax authority of tax, including payments of advance corporation tax and purchases of certificates of tax deposit.

(iv) Investing activities

The cash flows included in investing activities are those related to the acquisition or disposal of any asset held as a fixed asset or as a current asset investment (other than assets included within cash equivalents).

Cash inflows from investing activities include:

(a) receipts from sales or disposals of fixed assets
(b) receipts from sales of investments in subsidiary undertakings net of any balances of cash and cash equivalents transferred as part of the sale
(c) receipts from sales of investments in other entities with separate disclosure of divestments of equity accounted entities
(d) receipts from repayment or sales of loans made to other entities by the reporting entity or of other entities' debt (other than cash equivalents) which were purchased by the reporting entity.

Cash outflows from investing activities include:

(a) payments to acquire fixed assets
(b) payments to acquire investments in subsidiary undertakings net of balances of cash and cash equivalents acquired
(c) payments to acquire investments in other entities with separate disclosure of investments in equity accounted entities
(d) loans made by the reporting entity and payments to acquire debt of other entities (other than cash equivalents).

(v) Financing

Financing cash flows comprise receipts from or repayments to external providers of finance of amounts in respect of principal amounts of finance.
  Financing cash inflows include:

(a) receipts from issuing shares or other equity instruments
(b) receipts from issuing debentures, loans, notes, and bonds and from other long and short-term borrowings (other than those included within cash equivalents).

  Financing cash outflows include:

(a) repayments of amounts borrowed (other than those included within cash equivalents)
(b) the capital element of finance lease rental payments
(c) payments to re-acquire or redeem the entity's shares
(d) payments of expenses or commissions on any issue of shares, debentures, loans, notes, bonds or other financing.

  The amounts of any finance cash flows received from or paid to equity accounted entities should be disclosed separately.

EXCEPTIONAL AND EXTRAORDINARY ITEMS

Where cash flows relate to items that are classed as exceptional items in the profit and loss account these exceptional cash flows should be shown under the appropriate standard headings, according to the nature of each item. Sufficient disclosure of the nature of cash flows relating to exceptional items should be given in a note to the cash flow statement to allow a user of the financial statements to gain an understanding of the effect on the reporting entity's cash flows of the underlying transactions.

Where cash flows relate to items that are classed as extraordinary items in the profit and loss account these extraordinary cash flows should be shown separately under the appropriate standard headings, according to the nature of each item. In the extremely rare circumstances where it is inappropriate to include a cash flow relating to an extraordinary item under one or more of the standard headings within the cash flow statement the cash flows should be shown within a separate section in the cash flow statement.

Sufficient disclosures of the nature of cash flows relating to extraordinary items should be given in a note to the cash flow statement to allow a user of the financial statements to gain an understanding of the effect on the reporting entity's cash flows of the underlying transactions.

VALUE ADDED TAX AND OTHER TAXES

Cash flows should be shown net of any attributable Value Added Tax or other sales tax unless the tax is irrecoverable by the reporting entity. The net movement on the amount payable to, or receivable from, the taxing authority should be allocated to cash flows from operating activities unless a different treatment is more appropriate in the particular circumstances concerned. In circumstances where sales taxes paid by the reporting entity are irrecoverable, cash flows should be shown gross by including the associated sales tax unless this is impracticable, in which case the irrecoverable tax should be included under the most appropriate standard heading.

Taxation cash flows excluding those in respect of the reporting entity's revenue and capital profits and Value Added Tax, or other sales tax, should be included within the cash flow statement under the same standard heading as the cash flow which gave rise to the taxation cash flow, unless a different treatment is more appropriate in the particular circumstances concerned.

FOREIGN CURRENCIES

Where a portion of a reporting entity's business is undertaken by a foreign entity, the cash flows of that entity are to be included in the cash flow statement on the basis used for translating the results of those activities in the profit and loss account of the reporting entity.

HEDGING TRANSACTIONS

Cash flows that result from transactions undertaken to hedge another trans-action should be reported under the same standard heading as the transaction that is the subject of the hedge.

GROUPS

A group cash flow statement should only deal with flows of cash and cash equivalents external to the group. Accordingly, cash flows that are internal to the group should be eliminated in the preparation of the group cash flow statement. Dividends paid to any minority interests should be reported under the heading returns on investments and servicing of finance, and disclosed separately.

The cash flows of any entity which is equity accounted in consolidated financial statements should only be included in the group cash flow state-ment to the extent of the actual cash flows between the group and the entity concerned.

ACQUISITIONS AND DISPOSALS

Where a group acquires or disposes of a subsidiary undertaking, the amounts of cash and cash equivalents paid or received in respect of the consideration should be shown net of any cash and cash equivalent balances transferred as part of the purchase or sale of the subsidiary undertaking. In addition, a note to the cash flow statement should show a summary of the effects of acquisi-tions and disposals indicating how much of the consideration comprised cash and cash equivalents transferred as a result of the acquisitions and disposals.

Where a subsidiary undertaking joins or leaves a group during a financial year the cash flows of the group should include the cash flows of the sub-sidiary undertaking concerned for the same period as that for which the group's profit and loss account includes the results of the subsidiary under-taking.

Material effects on amounts reported under each of the standard headings reflecting the cash flows of a subsidiary undertaking acquired or disposed of in the period should be disclosed, as far as practicable, as a note to the cash flow statement. This information need only be given in the financial state-ments for the period in which the acquisition or disposal occurs.

MAJOR NON-CASH TRANSACTIONS

Material transactions not resulting in movements of cash or cash equivalents of the reporting entity should be disclosed in the notes to the cash flow statement if disclosure is necessary for an understanding of the underlying transactions.

RECONCILIATION WITH BALANCE SHEET FIGURES

The movements in cash and cash equivalents and the items shown within the financing section of the cash flow statement should be reconciled to the related items in the opening and closing balance sheets for the period. The reconciliations should disclose separately for cash and cash equivalents and for financing items the movements resulting from cash flows, differences arising from changes in foreign currency exchange rates (those relating to the retranslation of any opening balances of cash and cash equivalents and financing items and those resulting from the translation of the cash flows of foreign entities at exchange rates other than the year end rate) and other movements. Where several balance sheet amounts or parts thereof have to be combined to permit a reconciliation, sufficient detail should be shown to enable the movements to be understood. Possible formats for such reconciliations are provided in the illustrative examples annexed to the FRS.

COMPARATIVE FIGURES

Comparative figures should be given for all items in the cash flow statement and such notes thereto as are required by the FRS.

DATE FROM WHICH EFFECTIVE

The accounting practices set out in this FRS should be adopted as soon as possible and regarded as standard in respect of financial statements relating to accounting periods ending on or after 23 March 1992.

XYZ LIMITED
CASH FLOW STATEMENT FOR THE YEAR ENDED 31 MARCH 199X

	£'000	£'000
Net cash inflow from operating activities		6,889
Returns on investments and servicing of finance		
Interest received	3,011	
Interest paid	(12)	
Dividends paid	(2,417)	
Net cash inflow from returns on investments and servicing of finance		582
Taxation		
Corporation tax paid (including Advance Corporation Tax)	(2,922)	
Tax paid		(2,922)
Investing activities		
Payments to acquire intangible fixed assets	(71)	
Payments to acquire tangible fixed assets	(1,496)	
Receipts from sales of tangible fixed assets	42	
Net cash outflow from investing activities		(1,525)
Net cash inflow before financing		3,024
Financing		
Issue of ordinary share capital	211	
Repurchase of debenture loan	(149)	
Expenses paid in connection with shares issues	(5)	
Net cash inflow from financing		57
Increase in cash and cash equivalents		3,081

Notes to the cash flow statement

1. RECONCILIATION OF OPERATING PROFIT TO NET CASH INFLOW FROM OPERATING ACTIVITIES

	£'000
Operating profit	6,022
Depreciation charges	893
Loss on sale of tangible fixed assets	6
Increase in stocks	(194)
Increase in debtors	(72)
Increase in creditors	234
Net cash inflow from operating activities	6,889

2. ANALYSIS OF CHANGES IN CASH AND CASH EQUIVALENTS DURING THE YEAR

	£'000
Balance at 1 April 1991	21,373
Net cash inflow	3,081
Balance at 31 March 1992	24,454

	1992 £'000	1991 £'000	Change in year £'000
Cash at bank and in hand	529	681	(152)
Short-term investments	23,936	20,700	3,236
Bank overdrafts	(11)	(8)	(3)
	24,454	21,373	3,081

4. ANALYSIS OF CHANGES IN FINANCING DURING THE YEAR

	Share Capital £'000	Debenture loan £'000
Balance at 1 April 1991	27,411	156
Cash inflow/(outflow) from financing	211	(149)
Profit on repurchase of debenture loan for less than its book value	—	(7)
Balance at 31 March 1992	27,622	—

APPENDIX II: CORPORATE QUESTIONNAIRE

INTRODUCTION

This Appendix takes the format of a comprehensive check-list to serve as an aide-memoire to areas for corporate investigation. The list can be used in its entirety to aid production of a comprehensive corporate report; or you can simply select key areas from within the list as appropriate to the business situation you encounter.

QUESTIONNAIRE CHECK-LIST

Nature and history of the business

– What are the main activities of the business?
– When formed and trading structure
– Short precis of development to date
– Relationship with parent or subsidiary companies
– Main directors and shareholders
– Premises details

Current financial facilities

– Bank loans and overdrafts with schedule of repayment programme
– hire purchase/leasing
– other credit lines?

Management responsibilities and organisation

– Outline senior executives; age/experience etc.
– Is there an organisational chart?
– Are there gaps in key areas of management: general management; sales; production; finance and personnel?

– Are there recruitment, training and promotion plans?
– Can the management team cope with expansion of the business?
– Is each job clearly defined?
– Have they delegated routine tasks as far as possible?
– Are managers accountable for specific areas of responsibility?
– Are there clearly defined lines of reporting?
– Do they coordinate projects with a team responsibility?

Corporate objectives

– Has the company developed clear objectives, both short and long term?
– Are these objectives quantified in terms of market share; growth; product mix; rate of return?
– Are there review periods for the objectives?
– Have they developed a financial plan and technical plan from these objectives?
– Are the objectives realistic?
– What is the significance of the objectives relative to the capital base?
– Have they analysed the strengths and weaknesses of the business?
– Have they identified the limiting factors to the business?

Product marketing/sales targets

– What are the main factors affecting demand for products? Market competition; prices; quantities; seasonal trends?
– Are the product lines expanding or declining?
– Are there plans and research for follow-on products?
– Is there a well-spread customer base or is the company in the hands of one or two main customers?
– Do they monitor sales goods returned as defective?
– Do they review 'make' or 'buy-in' decisions?
– Are there specific sales areas defined and sales targets set?

Product production

– Do they plan production levels to link in with exports and sales?
– If sales are made from finished goods stock do they control lead-times correctly?
– Does the business have the physical production capability to meet planned sales?

- Are the premises adequate?
- Do they have job cards setting out raw material requirements and estimating labour/machines hours for specific products?
- Do they plan for effective production runs rather than piece-work?
- Do they monitor labour efficiency?
- Does the production controller liaise with the buyer to ensure an adequate, but not excessive, raw material stock?
- Do they monitor wastage of materials?
- Do they monitor defective goods returned?

Product pricing

- Are costs estimated first to give a guide-line to the price-setters?
- Are they careful in the giving of discounts for large orders or early payments?
- Do the cost estimates include an element for future inflation?
- Do they endeavour to find out what their competitors are charging?
- What is the minimum price for the product to achieve break-even?
- Do they frequently review prices?
- Do they undertake market research?

Stock control/purchase control

- What is the lead-time for the products?
- Are stocks kept up to a minimum acceptable level for operational needs?
- Pareto's principle of the 80/20 rule can be useful in stock control. Does 20% of their stock articles represent 80% of the total stock value?
- Do they have an effective stock control system?
- Do they carry out quarterly physical stock-takes as a measure of control?
- Do they have a monthly review of stock holding?
- How often are quotes obtained from new suppliers to check on purchasing prices?
- Can suppliers carry stock and make more frequent deliveries?
- Are they careful not to buy in large quantities just to obtain a discount?
- Do they have separate stock level guides for raw materials/work-in-progress and finished goods?
- Do they dispose of obsolete stock?
- Are the stocks insured?

Creditor control

– Is the policy to take credit for as long as possible or pay quickly?
– Do they take discounts when appropriate?
– Is there a monthly review of creditors by age analysis?
– Do they keep a close check on amounts owing to key suppliers?

Debtor control

– Do they nominate specific responsibilities?
– Is there a review monthly, using age analysis?
– Do they check on new customers for credit worthiness?
– What are the normal terms of trade?
– Are invoices despatched promptly?
– Do they send out statements regularly and quickly after the month-end?
– Is there a 'chase' letter system for outstanding debts?
– Do they take firm action against late payers?
– Can they get progress payments on large orders?
– Have they considered credit risk insurance?
– Do they 'code' key accounts?

Overheads control/analysis

– Is there an overheads budget?
– Do they monitor monthly against budget?
– Do they closely monitor by analysis of major overhead items?
– Do they set overhead costs targets to individual departments where appropriate?
– Do they know minimum sales to cover annual overheads?

Trading results (profit and loss and balance sheets)

– Analyse key ratios
– Summarise trends over several years
– What are the reasons for main fluctuations?

BUDGETS

Capital expenditure

– Do they draw up an annual budget and monitor monthly?
– Can payback of income etc. justify the outlay of cost?
– Is this budget brought forward into the cash budget?

Profit budget

– What is the projected net profit?
– Is this monitored on a monthly/quarterly basis?
– Do they nominate someone responsible for monitoring?
– Do they 'flex' the budget if circumstances change radically?
– Is the sales level being reached to cover break-even costs?
– Compare budget figures to results in last year's performance.

Cash budget

– Have they included all cash items including capital expenditure?
– Are they monitoring monthly?
– Do they reconcile with bank statement?
– Is the cash flow positive or negative and to what extent?

Funds flow

– Is the business a cash consumer or generator?
– What percentage of funds are generated from trading as opposed to external finance?
– Is funds flow projected for big projects?

Security

– Detail security lodged for advance. Is there a debenture mortgage charge?

Financial requirements

– What are the projected financial requirements in summary?
– Structure of finance e.g. overdraft; loan and repayment plan
– Comment on payback ability; capital gearing.

BIBLIOGRAPHY

E.I. du Pont de Nemours, The du Pont formula, 1950s

Robert Buchele, How to Evaluate a Firm, California Management Review, 1962, pp. 5–16

H.I. Ansoff, Corporate Strategy, Penguin, 1965

E.I. Altman, 'Financial Ratios, Discriminant Analysis and the Prediction of Corporate Bankruptcy', Journal of Finance, Vol. 23, No. 4, Sept 1968, pp. 589–609

E. Altman, Corporate Bankruptcy in America, Heath, Lexington, Mass., 1971

Andrews, The Formulation of Business Strategy, Harvard Business Review, 1971

Kotler, Stages of the Life Cycle, 1972

J. Argenti, Corporate Collapse: The Causes and Symptoms, McGraw-Hill, 1976

McKinsey & Co., Economic Value to the Customer, Forbus and Mehta, 1979

Michael Porter, Competitive Strategy: Techniques for Analysing Industries and Competitors, New York Free Press, 1980

S.A. Tucker, Profit Planning Decisions with Break-even Systems, Gower, 1980

D. Bibeault, Corporate Turnaround, McGraw-Hill, 1981

Edward I. Altman, 'The Success of Business Failure Prediction Models, An International Survey', Journal of Banking and Finance 8, 1984, pp. 171–198, North-Holland

S. Slatter, Corporate Recovery, Penguin, 1984

A. Bathory, The Analysis of Credit: Foundations and Development of Corporate Credit Assessment, McGraw-Hill, 1987

Boyadjian & Warren, Risks – Reading Corporate Signals, John Wiley & Sons, 1987

R.S. Norgard, 'The Causes of Corporate Collapse', Australian Accountant (Australia) Journal, Vol. 57, No. 3, April 1987, pp. 24–25

Anne H. Reilly, 'Are Organizations Ready for a Crisis? A Managerial Scorecard', Columbia Journal of World Business, Vol. 22, No. 1, Spring 1987, pp. 79–88

James M. Gahlon & Robert L. Vigeland, 'Early Warning Signs of Bankruptcy Using Cash Flow Analysis', The Journal of Commercial Bank Lending, Dec 1988

Philip S. Scherer, 'The Turnaround Consultant Steers Corporate Renewal', Journal of Management Consulting, c. 1988

Edward M. Schulman, 'Two Methods for a Quick Cash Flow Analysis', The Journal of Commercial Bank Lending, June 1988

Mark Stevens, 'Turning Around a Troubled Company', D&B Reports Journal, Vol. 36, No. 6, Nov/Dec 1988, pp. 50–51

Manchester Business School, Corporate Strategic Planning, 1988

William Enderlein, 'Credit Analysis: The Power of Cash-Flow Analysis', Commercial Lending Review, c.1989

T.H. Jury, Understanding Money in Business, FSMD, 1989

Christopher Kemball, 'Laura Ashley's Refinancing Plan', Acquisitions Monthly, Dec 1990, pp. 25–26

John R.F. Lehane, Timothy l'Estrange & Adrian Powles, International Financial Law Review (UK), June 1990, pp. 7–15

J. Brian O'Connell, 'How Inventory Appraisals Are Done', The Journal of Commercial Bank Lending, April 1990

Lawrence R. Werner, 'When Crisis Strikes use a Message Action Plan', Public Relations Journal, Vol. 46, No. 8, 1990, pp. 30–31

Kenneth A. Hiltz & Kristine M. Gail, 'Settling Corporate Workouts', Business Credit Journal, Vol. 93, No. 9, Oct 1991, pp. 8–10

Financial Times 22/2/91, Cash Flow Becomes the Determining Factor

Shelly Branch, 'Go with the flow – or else', Black Enterprise, Vol. 22, No. 4, Nov 1991, pp. 77–82

Dianne Hayes Casey, 'Cash Flows from Operations: Why it Deserves More Attention', Corporate Controller Journal, Vol. 4, No. 6, July/Aug 1992, pp. 46–48

T. Smith, Accounting for Growth, 1992

Financial Times 25/5/93, Hi-Tec Misses its Step

W.H. Beaver, 'Financial Ratios as Predictors of Failure', Journal of Accounting Research, Vol. 5, pp. 71–111

Annual accounts

Hi-Tec	1992	1993
JN Nichols (Vimto)	1991	1992
Laura Ashley	1990	

INDEX

Further titles of interest

FINANCIAL TIMES

PITMAN PUBLISHING

ISBN	TITLE	AUTHOR
0 273 60561 5	Achieving Successful Product Change	Innes
0 273 03970 9	Advertising on Trial	Ring
0 273 60232 2	Analysing Your Competitor's Financial Strengths	Howell
0 273 60466 X	Be Your Own Management Consultant	Pinder
0 273 60168 7	Benchmarking for Competitive Advantage	Bendell
0 273 60529 1	Business Forecasting using Financial Models	Hogg
0 273 60456 2	Business Re-engineering in Financial Services	Drew
0 273 60069 9	Company Penalties	Howarth
0 273 60558 5	Complete Quality Manual	McGoldrick
0 273 03859 1	Control Your Overheads	Booth
0 273 60022 2	Creating Product Value	De Meyer
0 273 60300 0	Creating World Class Suppliers	Hines
0 273 60383 3	Delayering Organisations	Keuning
0 273 60171 7	Does Your Company Need Multimedia?	Chatterton
0 273 60003 6	Financial Engineering	Galitz
0 273 60065 6	Financial Management for Service Companies	Ward
0 273 60205 5	Financial Times Guide to Using the Financial Pages	Vaitilingam
0 273 60006 0	Financial Times on Management	Lorenz
0 273 03955 5	Green Business Opportunities	Koechlin
0 273 60385 X	Implementing the Learning Organisation	Thurbin
0 273 03848 6	Implementing Total Quality Management	Munro-Faure
0 273 60025 7	Innovative Management	Phillips
0 273 60327 2	Investor's Guide to Emerging Markets	Mobius
0 273 60622 0	Investor's Guide to Measuring Share Performance	Macfie
0 273 60528 3	Investor's Guide to Selecting Shares that Perform	Koch
0 273 60704 9	Investor's Guide to Traded Options	Ford
0 273 03751 X	Investor's Guide to Warrants	McHattie
0 273 03957 1	Key Management Ratios	Walsh
0 273 60384 1	Key Management Tools	Lambert
0 273 60259 4	Making Change Happen	Wilson
0 273 60424 4	Making Re-engineering Happen	Obeng
0 273 60533 X	Managing Talent	Sadler
0 273 60153 9	Perfectly Legal Competitor Intelligence	Bernhardt
0 273 60167 9	Profit from Strategic Marketing	Wolfe
0 273 60170 9	Proposals, Pitches and Beauty Parades	de Forte
0 273 60616 6	Quality Tool Kit	Mirams
0 273 60336 1	Realising Investment Value	Bygrave
0 273 60713 8	Rethinking the Company	Clarke
0 273 60328 0	Spider Principle	Linton
0 273 03873 7	Strategic Customer Alliances	Burnett
0 273 03949 0	Strategy Quest	Hill
0 273 60624 7	Top Intrapreneurs	Lombriser
0 273 03447 2	Total Customer Satisfaction	Horovitz
0 273 60201 2	Wake Up and Shake Up Your Company	Koch
0 273 60387 6	What Do High Performance Managers Really Do?	Hodgson

For further details or a full list of titles contact:

The Professional Marketing Department, Pitman Publishing, 128 Long Acre, London WC2E 9AN, UK

Tel +44 (0)71 379 7383 or fax +44 (0)71 240 5771